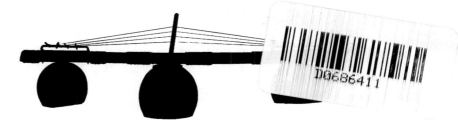

Mel Bay Presents

Play the World
The 101 World Instrument Primer
By Randy Raine-Reusch

1 2 3 4 5 6 7 8 9 0

Visit us on the Web at www.melbay.com — E-mail us at email@melbay.com

CD Contents

Introduction

The growing interest in world music has brought a wide range of musical instruments into our homes, either from our travels through the jungles or deserts of a distant country, or simply from the local music store. Although most people may be able to coax a sound or two from them, often they do not have the luxury of taking lessons, or even find correct information on the instruments. This book is a primer providing music, tunings, basic playing techniques, and background information on over one hundred world instruments. It would take many books to fully explain how to properly play the enclosed instruments, and some of these can take a lifetime to master. The attempt here is to introduce the instruments and get the player started. There are instruments included that may be readily available in one area while not in others, so many readers may discover a number of new instruments in these pages. Hopefully, with the assistance of the recordings, this book will be useful for most readers to start playing one or more instruments from their collections.

Notes on the recordings and scores

To fit all the pieces onto a single CD, recordings of the midjweh and arghul follow each other on a single track, as do the kalimba and mbira, as well as the musical glasses and musical saw. An effort has been made to provide an authentic sound and representational style for most of the instruments. The enclosed pieces range from traditional works and composed pieces similar to traditional works, to composed pieces in a more contemporary manner. All traditional pieces are labeled as such. In order to facilitate the reader, western tunings and notation are used throughout. However as many non-western instruments cannot be easily notated using the western staff system, there are instances when the notation is an approximation of what is played.

Acknowledgements

Sincere thanks go to the following for their assistance with this project:
Emad Armoush, Victor Chorobik, Joseph 'Pepe' Danza, Moshe Denburg, Michael Dunn, Itamar Erez, Graeme Gibson, Gordon Grdina, D'arcy Han, Sutrisno Hartana, Bich Ngoc Ho, Eclilson de Jesus, Amir Koushkani, Chris Miller, Dr. Terry Miller, Blessing Mubaiwa, Edgar Muenala, Dr. Phong Nguyen, Jay O'Keeffe, Milton Randall, Jun Rong, Rene Hugo Sanchez, Fana Soro, Don Xaliman, Zhi Min Yu, Wei Wang, Zhong Xi Wu. Very special thanks go to Mei Han for all her tireless work and dedication.

Photos by Randy Raine-Reusch and Mei Han, author photo by Tim Matheson, edited by Randy Raine-Reusch, Mei Han, and Don Xaliman. Transcriptions by Mei Han, Itamar Erez, Moshe Denburg and Randy Raine-Reusch. CD recorded by Yu Wei at Trinity Studios, Vancouver.

About the Author

Randy Raine-Reusch is a composer, international concert-artist, educator and world music specialist. He has studied music in over ten countries with numerous teachers, from headhunters to National Treasures. A prodigious multi-instrumentalist with a collection of over seven hundred instruments, Raine-Reusch has recorded and/or performed with the Tianjin Symphony Orchestra, Victoria Symphony Orchestra, Aerosmith, Yes, The Cranberries, Pauline Oliveros, Stuart Dempster, Jon Gibson, Barry Guy, Robert Dick, Frank Gratkowski, Mats Gustafsson, Sainkho Namtchylak, Jin Hi Kim, and the Japanese Iemoto, or Hereditary Grand Master, of Seikyodo Ichigenkin. Raine-Reusch has toured internationally as a solo artist, as leader of the world beat ensemble ASZA, or with Chinese zheng virtuoso Mei Han to many prestigious festivals and events, including two WOMAD festivals and three World Expos, on tours to Australia, Germany, Spain, Czech Republic, South Africa, China, India, Korea, Japan, Singapore, Vietnam, Malaysia and the Philippines. In addition to performing, Randy was the founder of the Rainforest World Music Festival in Sarawak, Malaysia; a consultant of the Stearn's Collection of Musical Instruments at the University of Michigan, Ann Arbor; and a consulting editor and writer for Musicworks Magazine. He has lectured on world music and instruments in many institutes around the world. More info is available at www.asza.com.

Instrumental Families

The instruments in this book are arranged by category and then by instrumental familes, with some related families grouped together.

STRINGS

Fiddles and Bowed Rebabs
Stick fiddles are common throughout Asia and are distinguished by long thin necks, piercing wood or hide covered resonators and a small number of bowed strings. Stick fiddles are usually played vertically in front of the musician. *Bowed rebabs* have either an animal hide or wooden top on wooden bodies with the sides cut away to make room for the bow. Over the centuries these definitions have blurred as in the case of the Indonesian rebab which is actually a stick fiddle.

Harps, Lyres, and Harp-Lutes
Harps and *lyres* were found in Mesopotamia from four to five thousand years ago and have since traveled throughout the world. *Harps* are found in three main forms: *frame harps* that have a resonant body on one side and a frame enclosing the strings, such as the Celtic harp; *arched harps* that have a resonant body and an arched neck with the strings going between, like those found in Africa and Asia; and *angular harps* with a neck at a sharp angle to the body and strings running between, like those of the ancient Greek harps. *Lyres* have a sound box, two arms, and a yoke or crossbar between the arms. The strings run from the end of the body across a small bridge, and then to the yoke. The distance between the body and the yoke can range from the length of a hand to over six feet or two meters. Lyres are still common in East Africa and parts of Eurasia. *Harp-lutes* are a separate classification of instrument found in West Africa that are constructed from a gourd intersected by a pole for a neck with the strings running from the end of the gourd across a large bridge to attach to the pole.

Lutes and Plucked Rebabs
Lutes are defined as plucked string instruments that have either a short or long neck attached to a body, in the same plane as the body. Also included here are instruments that are related to the lute family. *Rebabs* come under two classifications: plucked and bowed. There are many suggestions that originally all *rebabs* were bowed but over time some transformed to plucked instruments. As well, some instruments now found outside the rebab family, such as the guitar and violin, may have originally been *rebabs*, and some present day plucked rebabs are now closer to the lute family than to ancient rebabs. Also included here is the *boat lute* although it belongs to a separate instrument family altogether.

Zithers
Zithers are defined as string instruments without a neck and where the body runs the length of the strings. There are a number of types of zithers depending on the body shape and material. *Tube zithers* were usually made from bamboo, *stick zithers* from sticks, *board zithers* from boards or planks, *trough zithers* were usually carved from wood, *mat zithers* were woven, and *box zithers* which include long zithers had a wooden soundbox of varying sizes. Most zithers are plucked but some are hammered or bowed.

WINDS

Flutes

Anything that is wind blown without a reed is included in this section, from *end-blown flutes* (blown from the end), *oblique flutes* (blown at an angle), *transverse flutes* (blown from the side), *nose flutes* (blown with the nose), *panpipes*, and *ocarinas*. Some flutes, like recorders, have a fipple or duct that sounds when air is passed over, others, like the western concert flute, only sound when air passes over a sharp edge on the end or side.

Free Reeds

Free reeds are instruments that have a reed placed flush with the wall of a resonating tube and are found in two forms: *mouth organs* and *single melodic pipes*. *Mouth organs* have many pipes surrounded by a wind chamber. Each pipe only sounds one pitch upon inhalation or exhalation and the pitch is changed by sounding another pipe. A s*ingle melodic pipe* has fingerholes to change the pitch and the reed only blows in one direction. The Asian free reed family was brought to Europe in the eighteenth century to give birth to the harmonica, accordion, reed organ, and concertina.

Horns

Almost any long tube or chamber with a hole on either end can be used as a horn. *Conch shell* and *empty log horns* are found almost worldwide. Horns are usually, but not always, played with a firm embouchure that is tightened to play higher notes. Horns make use of a tube's overtone series to produce the pitches, which means that the longer the tube is, the easier it is to play melodic passages, which is why the long *Swiss alpenhorn* is far more versatile than the conch. However shorter instruments such as *signal horns* tend to have much more volume.

Reeds

Reed instruments are some of the oldest instruments in the world and are basically divided into single and multiple vibrating reeds. *Single reeds* are usually members of the *clarinet* family, and *multiple reeds* belong to the *shawm* family. Although there are many multiple reeds, only double reed instruments are included here. In both the single and multiple reed families, body shapes can be either tubular or conical, with the latter having the loudest instruments. Many traditional reed instruments require circular breathing; please refer to *Circular Breathing* in the *Playing Techniques* section.

PERCUSSION and MORE

Drums, Balafons, Rattles, Scrapers

Percussion instruments can include just about anything that makes a sound when it is shaken, rubbed, scraped, or struck. As a result, percussion instruments, more than any other genre, demonstrate a wealth of human ingenuity applied to the creation of musical instruments.

Jaw Harps or Jews Harps

The term *jews harp* is quite controversial, due to racial associations, so many people now prefer to use the term *jaw harp*. There is also a discussion about whether jaw harps are percussion or free reeds instruments. Nevertheless, there are two main categories of jaw harps: metal and fibre, both are found worldwide. *Fibre jaw harps* can be made from wood, bamboo or palm stem and are further subdivided by the method of activation: tension and plucked. Jaw harps are usually constructed with a frame and a *lamella*, or tongue, as the sounding device. Jaw harps are put in front of the performer's mouth to increase the volume and to shift the tone by movements of the lips, tongue and oral cavity. *Tension jaw harps* are activated by jerking a string connected to the lamella, in contrast to most jaw harps, which are plucked.

Musical Bows

Musical bows originated in Africa and are considered one of the world's first instruments. They are played by plucking, striking or bowing, and use either a gourd or the performer's mouth as a resonator. *Struck bows*, found in Africa and South America, use a gourd resonator held close to the performer's body, which creates a *wah* effect when moved away from the players chest. Bows that use the mouth as a resonator are found in the eastern US, Central America, South America, parts of Oceania, southern Taiwan, and Africa. *Mouth bows* may have a single undivided string, a single string divided into two, or multiple strings. Mouth bows are either plucked, or bowed and are extremely quiet instruments used for personal entertainment rather than performance. Most mouth bows are held so that the back of one end of the bow-stave is held against the player's cheek very close to the mouth, and the lips, palette and tongue are manipulated to enforce the overtones of the bow string. In some regions, performers place the bowstring close to the open mouth to produce the harmonics. Single undivided-string bows, like those common in the US, are plucked at the far end of the bow either by a plectrum or the fingers, and sometimes the bow is compressed to lower the pitch.

Others

This section includes a number of instruments that simply fall through the cracks of the main categories. The *kalimba* and *mbira* are known as *lamellaphones* or instruments with tongues. The *musical glasses* and *saw* are both a type of friction instrument, but are obviously quite different.

Special Playing Techniques

Circular Breathing

Circular breathing is a technique of taking air in through the nose at the same time as blowing air out of the mouth, allowing a wind instrument a continuous stream of air supply. It is common on *didjeridu*, single and double reeds and some flutes. There are basically two steps to circular breathing. **Step One**: breathe out of the mouth while keeping the cheeks puffed. **Step Two**: take a very quick breath in through the nose while using the cheek muscles to push the stored air in the cheeks out through the mouth. Step one is easy, as long as there is air in the cheeks and they do not collapse, even if the lungs are empty. Step two takes a bit of practice.

First practice filling your mouth with water and not swallowing it, then breathe in and out through your nose. Then with the water still in your mouth, empty your lungs through your nose and hold - don't breathe in, then breathe in through your nose and at the same time spit the water out of your mouth in a long thin stream by pushing with your cheeks. Practice spitting water out of your mouth and breathing in through your nose at the exact same time, until this becomes easy and comfortable. Now fill your mouth with air and hold it as you did the water, and then push the air out of your mouth while breathing in through your nose. This is exactly the same process as with water in your mouth, and may again take a bit of practice. Once you are comfortable with it, then add step one. Breathe out of your mouth with cheeks puffed, and then quickly close off the air supply to your mouth without collapsing your cheeks, then do step two by breathing in through your nose and pushing the air in your cheeks out, and then repeat the process till smooth. The trick is to take a very fast and short breath in through your nose, as your cheeks do not store much air. Practice by blowing air on your hand until you feel that it doesn't stop, but be aware that the transition between steps one and two takes a while to make smooth. Once you feel that you are circular breathing then try it on a *didjeridu*, again you will find that the transition takes awhile. Often it is a good idea to practice circular breathing while watching TV, as it is easier when your brain is not involved and TV is very good for turning off your brain. Please be aware that some instruments are very challenging to circular breath on.

Tonguing
Tonguing is a form of articulation used on wind instruments performed by quickly touching the back of teeth or hard palette with the tongue effectively interrupting the air stream, as in saying 'da' or 'ta'. *Double tonguing* alternates between a 'ta' and a 'ka', whereas *triple tonguing* uses 'ta-ka-ta' repeatedly.

Raising a Tone with the Thumb
This is a technique used for raising a pitch on a harp by using a thumb or fingernail to press against a string lightly, very close to the soundboard or neck while the other hand plucks the string. It is a common technique on Burmese and South American harps. The note is often very short and used as a grace note for ornamentation.

Muting
Muting with the base of the hand is common on many string instruments, both as the string is being plucked (charango), or just after it is plucked (kayagum), to get either a more rhythmic or staccato sound. Muting is quite dynamic and variations on the timing, the amount and the duration of a mute, can create a wide range of stunning effects.

Hammer-on and Pull-off
These are common techniques for fretted instruments. While a finger is pressing a string against a fret, perform a *hammer-on* by forcefully hammering an adjacent finger on to the next higher fret on the same string so it sounds without plucking the string. A *pull-off* is performed by then pulling this finger off so that the finger plucks the string. These two techniques are often alternated repeatedly at a variety of speeds. Hammer-ons and pull-offs produce a subtle sound, yet an essential one to a number of instruments.

Rapid Picking
Many Middle Eastern and Central Asian lutes have a very distinctive picking style that produces a very fast tremolo with a plectrum. The western version of this technique is used on the mandolin where the plectrum is held between the thumb and the first two fingers, with the wrist and forearm moving as a single unit and the elbow as the fulcrum. However, the Middle Eastern and Central Asian style is quite different. The wrist is bent to almost a right angle to the forearm and is held extremely loose, so that it moves rapidly back and forth. The forearm is tight and the elbow is again used as a fulcrum. This latter technique is frowned on in the West, as it can be quite hard on the forearm and wrist joint. The result, though, creates a very fast and distinctive tremolo.

Rapid Picking Without a Plectrum
Strumming rapidly without a plectrum is common on a wide range of instruments from the charango to the dombra, although there are a number of different approaches. The most common technique uses the top of the index finger as if it was a pick, by bracing the first joint on either side with the thumb and middle finger, and striking the string in both directions with sides of the finger. Another common technique alternates the index finger and thumb, with the finger striking on the down stroke and the thumb on the upstroke, although on some instruments this order is reversed. A third technique uses some or all of the fingers striking the strings in succession in either an up or down stroke, often alternating with a thumb stroke in the opposite direction. Many people are familiar with the Flamenco version of this technique, yet there are many variations depending on the number of fingers used, how close they are to each other, the direction of the fingers, and how the thumb is used if at all.

The Instruments

Erhu - China

The erhu is the most common two-string stick fiddle of China. The name translates roughly to the words *two* and *barbarian*, as it came to China from the tribal peoples of the north approximately a thousand years ago. The modern erhu has two metal strings that are very close to each other, a thin wooden neck and a round tubular body covered with python skin. The horse-hair bowstrings are woven between the two strings. The erhu is a very popular instrument and can be found in almost all forms of music in China.

Playing the Erhu
The erhu is played while seated and held in the left hand with the body rest-ing on the left thigh so that the skin top faces at a slight angle away from the centre of the player's lap. The bow is held so that the player's second and third fingers are touching the bow hairs and creating tension on them with a light pressure. The bow is pushed slightly away from the performer's body when playing the outside string, and pulled towards the body to play the inside string. Both strings are fretted lightly at the same time, enabling a wide range of expressive vibrato, slides, melismatic colourations, and virtuosic passages.

Tuning the Erhu

The erhu is usually tuned to a fifth (d, a), with the higher string the farther from the body when the instrument is held. Fine tuners are now available for the instrument to aid in tuning, and there are even devices to change tun-ing rapidly with a flick of a switch.

Jasmine Flower TRACK 1   Traditional

9

Goge - West Africa

The goge is the one string stick fiddle of the savanna region of West Africa found in a variety of shapes and sizes, and known by a number of names. Typically, goge are made from a lizard skin covered half gourd, pierced by a thin neck and a horsehair string that passes over a small bridge placed close to the edge of the gourd. Bowed with a small horsehair bow, the goge has a very distinctive sound that makes use of a multiphonic voice. Played by both men and women with great virtuosity, the goge is used in small ensembles and to accompany singing.

Playing the Goge

The body of the goge rests on the player's lap with the top facing up and the neck pointing away from the performer's body horizontally. The bow's position must be adjusted away from the bridge to play the lower octave only, or closer to the bridge to play the characteristic split octave sound. Varying the bow pressure also greatly assists in obtaining the desired sound.

Tuning the Goge
As it only has one string, the goge is simply tuned to the singer's voice. The string is tied to the neck with hide and therefore must be pushed or pulled along the neck to tune. If the string slips, a small amount of lemon juice should be applied to the neck.

Orono

(play close the bridge to get split harmonics)

Koni - Vietnam

The koni originated as a one-string fiddle from the Jorai people of the Central Highlands of Vietnam that was adopted by the music conservatories and transformed into a two-string instrument. The koni is unique in that it does not have a resonating chamber or sound box. In its place are two silk threads attached to the bottom of the strings, which run to a small bamboo or plastic disc that is held in the player's mouth. In this way the mouth acts as the resonating chamber, providing a vocal quality to the sound. The koni is performed as either a solo instrument or in small ensembles.

Playing the Koni

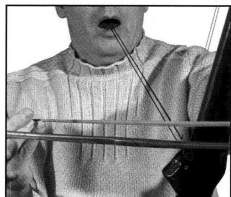

Traditionally, the koni was played resting the end on the ground with the player kneeling over it. However modern instruments are gripped between the knees while seated. The resonator disc is gripped between the teeth just behind the player's incisors and held so that the silk threads connecting it to the instrument are taut. Through precise movements of the lips and tongue, mimicking talking, the player can create an array of tonal colours that give the koni it's unique sound. The bow is held in the right hand with two fingers on the bowstrings to create tension.

Tuning the Koni

The koni is tuned to a fifth and adjusted for a comfortable string tension or to other instruments. If the strings are too loose or too tight, the instrument may not sound well.

On The Mountian Top   TRACK 3   Traditional

Rebab - Java, Indonesia

The Javanese rebab is a two-string spike fiddle used in the gamelan orchestra. It has a long wooden neck with two very long pegs inserted at right angles. The neck pierces a triangular shaped wooden body covered on one side with buffalo intestine. The bow passes over both strings. It is a very quiet but elegant instrument that often doubles or answers a singer. Increasingly, the rebab is used in small contemporary ensembles in the west.

Playing the Rebab

The rebab is rested on its spike on the floor and held upright in front of the performer. A good tone is dependent on a firm but light touch on the strings in addition to a steady tension created on the bowstrings by the fingers. Rather than rotating the bow to play individual strings, the instrument is rotated slightly. A slight tremolo is quite common.

Tuning the Rebab

The rebab is tuned to either a fourth or fifth, depending on the piece, and the inside string is tuned to the tonic of the scale used. As the pegs are quite delicate, tuning slightly above the note and pulling the string to stretch the string into tune is common.

Tiga COMPACT disc DIGITAL AUDIO TRACK 4   Traditional

(drone)

Sarinda - Nepal

The sarinda is a four-string bowed, horned rebab from Nepal. It was used by Gandharvas, a caste of wandering musicians, to carry the news and tell stories of the history of Nepal as they traveled between villages. The sarinda is carved from a single piece of wood with an opening on the upper part of the body while the lower part is covered in sheepskin. The four strings run across the bridge, which is placed at an oblique angle on the skin with the top edge resting on the side of the body. Modern sarinda have gut strings except for the top string, which is metal.

Playing the Sarinda
The sarinda can either be played sitting or standing. If sitting then the instrument is held upright with the tail of the instrument resting on the player's left thigh and the top of the instrument resting against the chest. If standing, a small cord or cloth belt is tied around the waist of the instrument and hooked into the player's belt to hold the instrument at waist height. In addition to bowing, many percussive sounds are produced on the sarinda, including plucking the strings and tapping on the instrument with either the fingers or the bow. Often bells are attached to the tip of the bow.

Tuning the Sarinda
The two center strings of the sarinda are tuned to the tonic and adjusted to match the singer's range. The top string is tuned a fifth higher and the lowest string a fourth lower (e.g. c,f,f,c1).

Kailash

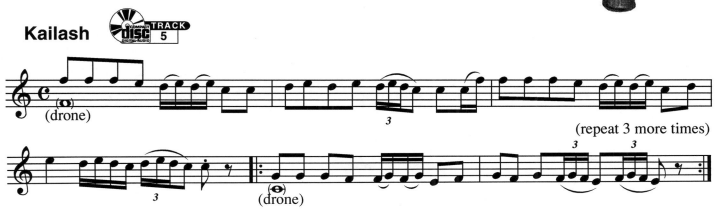

13

Ekidongo, Ennenga, or Adungu - Uganda

The ekidongo is the arched harp of the Nyoro people of Uganda, although variations are common throughout the region and played by a number of other cultures. The ekidongo has eight strings that run from a center strip along the body that attach to tuning pegs along the arched neck. The deep wooden body is covered with animal hide and distinguished by the multiple lacings. Traditionally used in small ensembles or to accompany a singer, the ekidongo has become a solo instrument of virtuosity.

Playing the Ekidongo
The body of the instrument is held on the lap with the arch pointing slightly away to the left. The right hand plays on the outside of the strings while the left on the inside. There are a number of techniques that vary per performer, such as the fingers of both hands carrying a melody on the higher strings while the thumbs carry a counterpoint on the lower strings, or the left hand in a high position playing a melody to the right hand's countermelody on the lower strings. Often a tremolo is achieved by rapidly plucking a string with alternating fingers from each hand.

Tuning the Ekidongo

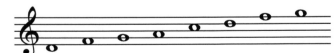

The gut strings are tuned to either a pentatonic or diatonic scale and adjusted to either a singer's voice, or to a comfortable tension.

Mabira Night

Nyatiti - Kenya

The nyatiti, played by the Boma people, is the Kenyan version of the African lyre. Lyres are found throughout the east coast of Africa in a wide variety of sizes and with different names. Although lyres are said to have originated in Mesopotamia, the greatest number of these instruments are now found in eastern Africa. African lyres often have flat bridges that cause the strings to buzz, and sometimes musicians will also attach rattles to the instrument to increase the non-pitched sounds. African lyres come with five or more strings, with eight-string versions being quite common. They are usually played to accompany singing.

Playing the Nyatiti
The nyatiti is played positioned on its side either on the lap or floor, with the flat top facing away from the player and the crossbar to the left. The right hand reaches over the top to play the four bottom strings and the left hand plays the four top strings from the back. It could also be played on the floor with the player facing the instrument, and occasionally tapping on the sidebar with a coin held between their toes. Typical nyatiti music stresses repeated patterns that are essentially more rhythmic than melodic.

Tuning the Nyatiti

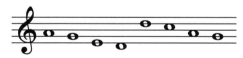

There are a number of tunings of the nyatiti, depending on the region and singer, but most are in pentatonic scales. The strings are attached to a long strip of cloth that is wrapped around the crossbar, and adjusting the tuning is done by gripping this cloth tightly in the hollow between the thumb and first finger, turning slightly to sharpen. Flattening the string is often best done by simply pulling on the string repeatedly.

Malindi

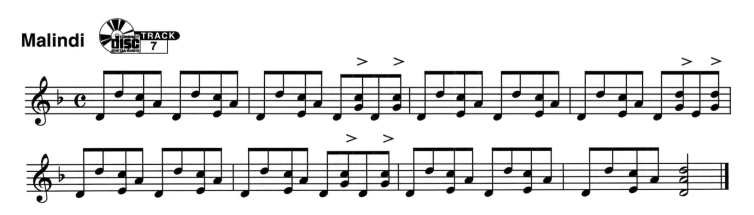

Saung Gauk - Burma (Myanmar)

The saung gauk is the sixteen-string arched harp of Burma or Myanmar. It is an elegant instrument adorned with red and black lacquer and gold leaf, yet the buyer must be aware that there are many imitation tourist quality instruments being sold that are simply ornamental. The saung gauk is traditionally used as an instrument of virtuosity, in ensembles or to accompany singing.

Playing the Saung Gauk

The saung gauk has a rich repertoire and incorporates many subtle techniques, therefore it is best learned under the guidance of a good teacher. It is held almost sideways on the lap facing to the left, with part of the strings and body underneath the right arm. The right hand plays on the outside of the strings while the left plays the inside. A characteristic technique of the saung gauk is for the left hand to raise a string a semi-tone or tone by pressing the left thumb nail on the string, close to the neck. A variation of this technique can also be used to quickly ornament or mute a note.

Tuning the Saung Gauk

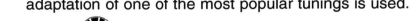

Traditional saung gauk are a tremendous headache to tune even for experienced artists. The strings are attached to ropes tied around the neck, and these ropes are knotted in a specific manner so that they will not slip. To adjust the tuning of a string, the knot must be loosened, the string tightened and then held while the knot is tightened again. The problem is that this will often put adjacent strings out of tune. Although modern instruments use tuning pegs, tuning can still be a bit arduous. There are numerous tunings for the saung gauk and almost all of them use intervals not found in the west. To make things easier for the beginner, a western adaptation of one of the most popular tunings is used.

Erawan TRACK 8

Biwa - Japan

The biwa is the Japanese teardrop lute used in court music or to accompany epic poems. The biwa originated from the Chinese pipa and came to Japan as a gift from the Chinese Tang court (618-907 AD). These original Chinese instruments are still preserved at the Shoso-in Imperial Repository in Nara, Japan. With either four or five strings, there are five main varieties of biwa, each with its own history, function, shape, and techniques. These are the *Gaku biwa* used in Gagaku or court music, the *Moso biwa* used by blind monks, the *Satsuma biwa* originally used by samurai, the *Heike biwa* used for reciting the epic poem of Heike, and the *Chikusen biwa*, which is the most modern and common. The Moso biwa style has effectively disappeared.

Playing the Biwa
Biwa are held in one of two positions either vertically or horizontally more like a guitar. Biwas are played with a plectrum, called a *batchi,* made from wood, bamboo, ivory or tortoise shell. Batchi vary in size and thickness depending on the style: the Satsuma batchi is distinctive at almost two-thirds the width of the

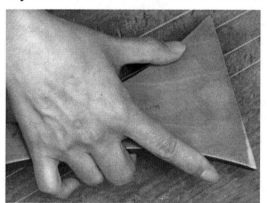

instrument, while the Chikuzen batchi is much smaller but thicker. How the batchi is held, varies with each style but usually the thumb is placed close to the top corner of the batchi and sometimes the little finger is on the opposite side of the handle to the rest of the fingers. The strings are struck with the corners of the batchi, the outstroke being quite easy, but the backstroke is more challenging and care must be taken to not catch the corner of the batchi on the string. A tremolo is possible but with extreme difficulty. In some styles, sound effects are created by sliding the batchi down the length of the strings, or quickly rubbing the strings with the edge of the batchi. Some pitches on the biwa can only be produced by pressing the string into the space between the frets to raise the pitch.

Tuning the Biwa
Each type of biwa has its own tunings although the pitch center is not standardized and is often varied to suit a singer's voice. Gaku biwa are played in 7 modes, each with its own tuning. The first of which is A,d,e,a; Heike biwa are tuned approximately A,c♯,e,a or G,B,d,g; the Satsuma tuning is G,d,g,a or G,d,g,d; and Chikuzen four string tuning is A,d,a,a and the five string tuning is D,A,d,e,a. The two thinnest strings are usually tuned in unison and played as one string. Care is taken not to tune the strings too high, as it is essential for the strings to be loose enough to produce the characteristic buzz of the strings.

Introduction to Shizuka Gozen TRACK 9   Traditional

17

Charango - Peru, Bolivia

The charango is a small Andean lute that was traditionally made from the body of an armadillo. There are a number of types and sizes with four to fifteen strings, and a wide range of tunings. The most common Charango has ten strings arranged in double courses. The charango is usually performed in a small ensemble with guitar and flutes to accompany singing. The fiery technique and rhythms of the charango have made it a very popular world instrument.

Playing the Charango
The charango is as percussive as it is melodic. Often, very complex staccato rhythms are played in chords with a characteristic strumming technique similar to the Flamenco guitar (see Rapid Picking). It is also common to dampen the strings while strumming and percussing on the top of the instrument.

There are a wide range of tunings and string arrangements for the charango. The most popular is in A minor from low to high: GG, c1c1, e2e1, a1a1, e2e2."

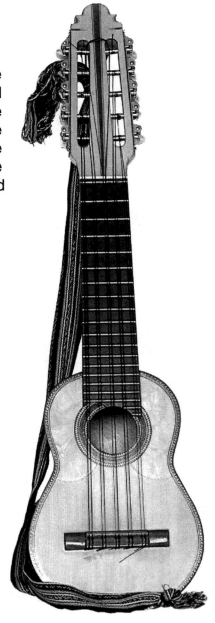

Carnaval de Tinta   TRACK 10   Traditional

1st repeat from measure 1
2nd repeat from Capo with variations

18

Dombra - Kazakhstan, Russia

The dombra is a pear shaped long necked lute of the Kazakh people of Central Asia. It has a slender long neck with fourteen gut frets and two gut strings. The dombra was traditionally used to accompany epic poems and folk songs, but now virtuosic instrumental pieces are also common. As a result, dombra have become a popular instrument with non-Kazakh peoples throughout Central Asia, Russia and in dombra clubs in the United States.

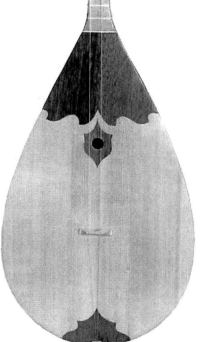

Playing the Dombra
The dombra is played without a plectrum and is strummed quite rapidly with the index finger, or with the index finger and thumb. Held so that the neck faces to the left, the left thumb, an important part of playing the dombra, actively frets the upper string while the fingers fret the lower string.

Tuning the Dombra
The dombra is usually tuned to a fourth within the range of the performer's voice. As the strings are fairly thick compared to other long neck lutes, care should be given to not tune them too high.

Issyk-Kul TRACK 11

(continue with variations)

Dutar - Xinjian, China

The dutar or *dotar* is a two-string long neck lute found in western China and Central Asia. There are many different types from the simple gut or silk string Uyghur instrument to the metal strung Afghan dutar with its many sympathetic strings. The term dutar comes from the Persian word for string *tar*, and the older Persian word for the number two *du*, now *do*. Dutar are found in a range of sizes with Uyghur dutar varying from one to three yards or meters in length. Dutar are used in ensemble music, as instruments of virtuosity, and to accompany singing.

Playing the Dutar
Some performers play the melody only on one string using the other as a drone, while others will also fret the second string with their thumb. The short dutar is usually played in a very rapid and energetic style with either with the fingers or with a plectrum. The longer dutar is usually played slower due to the awkwardness of fretting such a long instrument and the looseness of the string.

Tuning the Dutar
Commonly, the two strings are tuned in unison; or to a major second, a fourth or a fifth varying with the instrumentalist. Often the strings are the same gauge, and as they are made of gut or more commonly raw silk, great care must be taken not to break a string. Usually dutar have movable nylon or gut frets that are adjusted to play a particular mode or scale, which sometimes include quartertones.

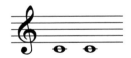

Xishan TRACK 12

20

Gimbri, Guimbri, or Sintir - Morocco

The gimbri or sintir is a three stringed rectangular lute from Morocco commonly used by Gnawan musicians. The body of the gimbri is a rectangular trough covered by camel skin from which protrudes a round wooden neck with three goat-gut strings attached by cloth thongs. At the end of the neck a metal rattle is inserted to give the instrument added color. The gimbri produces a percussive bass-like tone, and is the largest in a family of similar instruments found in Northern Africa.

Playing the Gimbri

The gimbri is both a percussive and melodic instrument. The knuckles of the right hand hit the skin on the body, while striking the bottom string with the index finger, or plucking the top and middle strings with the thumb. Done properly, this technique will simultaneously produce the tone of the string, a drum sound on the skin, and rattle the jingles on the end of the neck. Advanced players produce complex combinations of rhythms and melodies by varying these three elements.

Tuning the Gimbri

The gimbri is traditionally tuned to the musician's voice and within the tension level of the strings. Musicians who try to tune the gimbri to fit with other instruments often break strings by tuning them to high, so caution is advised. Held like a guitar, the thickest string on the gimbri is the top string and is tuned to the tonic, the thinnest string is in the center tuned an octave above the top string, and the last string on the bottom is tuned a fourth above the tonic. The method of adjusting the tuning is rather difficult. The player puts the end of the gimbri on the floor with the neck pointing into their chest. Then while placing their foot on the end of the body, they pull the cloth to which the string is attached towards them with their fingers to raise the pitch. To lower the pitch, slightly tap on the cloth in the direction of the instrument body. This is an awkward yet delicate job that takes practice. If the cloth slips often, apply a very small amount of lemon juice to the neck around the cloth.

Massa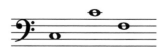

(repeat with variations)

Oud or Ud - Middle East

Common throughout the Arab and Persian world, the oud is a fret-less short-neck lute with a pear-shaped, flat top, rounded back, and a peghead characteristically bent backwards at a very sharp angle. The oud's origins are unknown, although myths attribute either celestial or magical beginnings, it more likely came from ancient Persia. The ancient oud, also referred to as a barbat, spread throughout the Middle East, into Europe to become the lute, and across the Silk Road to become the Chinese pipa, and Japanese biwa. The oud is now found in a wide variety of musical styles from accompanying the singing of epic poems, to orchestral music, and from Persian maqams to rock and jazz. Of the numerous styles of traditional oud the most advanced are Persian, Arabic and Turkish styles, each with a plethora of modes and scales, a complex music philosophy, and highly developed techniques.

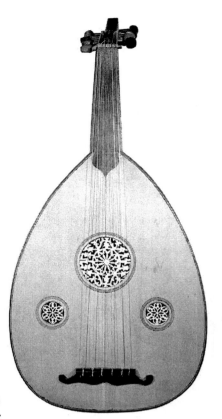

Playing the Oud
Holding the oud can be awkward at first because of the instrument's large belly. The neck is held in the left hand and the right arm either reaches over from the top or end. Usually, a very long pliable plectrum is used, typically made from a tortoise shell, while shirt stays or a piece cut from a plastic bottle are not unknown. In many regions, the oud plays in quartertones, and unless the player has grown up hearing these or has spent a substantial amount of time studying this music, quartertones are very difficult to play. However there are cultures that do not use quartertones on the oud so the performer has a choice of styles. As the oud is fretless, sliding in and out of notes and portamenti are characteristic. Very rapid hammer-ons and pull-offs are very common as well. Yet, the most distinctive playing technique is a style of extremely rapid tremolo described briefly in the *Rapid Picking* section.

Tuning the Oud
The oud has anywhere from eight to thirteen strings, usually strung in double courses of unison or octave pairs. Ouds with odd number of strings usually have a single bass string. There are a large number of modes, each with its own tuning, and as a result, there are a vast number of tunings for the oud that vary with Persian, Turkish or Arabic approaches to the instrument. Popular tunings for ten string ouds are low to high GG,AA,dd,gg,c1c1, and FF,AA,dd,gg,c1c1. Add a D and C respectively before the previous two tunings for eleven or twelve string ouds.

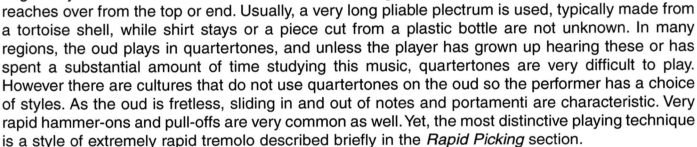

Brown Eyed Woman 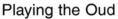 TRACK 14

Traditional

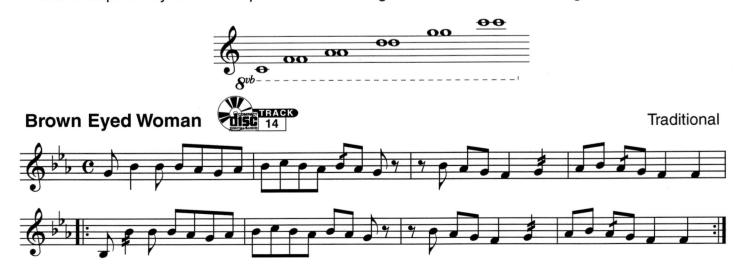

22

Pipa - China

The Pipa is the large pear-shaped teardrop lute of China. The pipa descended from the Persian *oud*, and was introduced to China around the 4th century. There are many depictions of early pipa in Tang Dynasty orchestras in the murals on the *Dun Huang* caves in western China that show a flattened instrument with just a few frets. Original instruments came in both four and five string versions, but over the centuries pipa have been standardized to four strings, while greatly increasing the number of frets. Classical pipa techniques and repertoire were well established before the 19th century, however in the 20th century, China's politicized modernization of traditional instruments transformed the pipa into a dynamic instrument of virtuosity. Pipa are now not only a prominent Chinese instrument in both small and large ensembles, but are increasingly found around the world in World Music, New Music, symphonic music, and jazz.

Playing the Pipa

The pipa is held upright on the lap in front of the left shoulder, with the strings facing away from the performer. The left hand balances and frets the instrument, while the right hand plucks. Nails

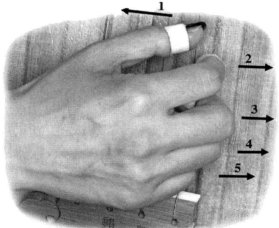

are worn on the thumb and all the fingers of the right hand. There are two basic picking techniques on the pipa, the first is an outward stroke (away from the palm) of the index finger which makes a *pi* sound, followed by an inward counterclockwise stroke with the thumb on the same string which makes the *pa* sound (hence the name pipa). A roll or tremolo is achieved by rapidly alternating these two. A faster and longer tremolo is produced by striking the strings rapidly in order from the index finger to the littler finger, followed by an inward counterclockwise stroke of the thumb. To effectively create a smooth continuous sound, this technique will take a substantial amount of practice.

Tuning the Pipa

The pipa has a standardized tuning of A,d,e,a.

Baban 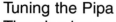 TRACK 15

Traditional

Rebab - Afghanistan

The Afghani rebab is a short-waisted, horned rebab with a goatskin top and a very deep body. Although there are a number of different sizes, all Afghani rebabs have three main strings, two to four drone strings and a number of sympathetic strings. The national instrument of Afghanistan, the Afghani rebab is also found in Pakistan and surrounding regions. It is used in small ensembles as a solo instrument, or to accompany vocal music. The Afghani rebab is a forerunner of the Indian *sarod*.

Playing the Rebab
The rebab is played horizontally on the lap balancing it on the right leg to enable the player's hand to move up the body on the melody strings. The characteristic Middle Eastern style of tremolo is often used (see *Rapid Picking*). Although there are only three or four frets on the rebab, it can also be played above the last fret on the highest melody string, which increases the instruments range and allows for characteristic sliding between notes.

Tuning the Rebab
The three melodic strings of the rebab are usually tuned to the tonic, fourth, and octave of the tonic. The drone strings are tuned to the tonic and fifth. The sympathetic strings are tuned to the pitches of the mode chosen to perform in.

Shikra CD TRACK 16

(repeat with variations)

Ruan - China

The ruan is a round-bodied four-string lute from China also referred to as a *moon guitar*. It should not be confused with yue-qin, which is a smaller folk instrument. The ruan's origins can be traced to China more than 2000 years ago. It is the parent to round bodied lutes found in Vietnam and Cambodia (Kampuchea). The ruan now comes in three sizes, the *da ruan* or bass ruan, the *zhong ruan* or mid-sized, and *xiao ruan*, the smallest. The ruan has a sweet mellow tone, reminiscent of the guitar, and is usually played in ensembles as an accompanying instrument.

Playing the Ruan
The ruan is held vertically on the left thigh with the strings facing forward. It is plucked with either a tortoise shell plectrum or with nails like those used for pipa. The ruan has a sound reminiscent of the guitar and can play single strings or chords.

Tuning the Ruan
The ruan is usually tuned tonic-fourth or tonic-fifth: A1,D,A,d or G1,D,G,d.

Torch Festival  TRACK 17   Traditional

Sapeh - Malaysia

The sapeh, also known as *sampet* or *sape*, is the boat lute found in the interior of northern Borneo, played by the Kenyah, Kayan, Kejamin, Iban, and Bidayuh peoples. With anywhere from three to five strings, sapehs are carved from a single piece of wood, with the back hollowed out, resembling a dugout canoe. Sapehs were traditionally played in pairs to accompany both men's and women's dances in the longhouse. The sapeh has recently grown in popularity, becoming the representative instrument of the Malaysian state of Sarawak in northern Borneo, and performed at almost every function or festival.

Playing the Sapeh
The sapeh is held on the lap like a guitar, even though fretting the instrument is quite awkward in this position. Only one string is fretted to play the melody. The other strings provide rhythmic accompaniment and are not played constantly as drones, but are played in a steady rhythmic ostinato interspersed between the melodic lines. Sapeh melodies are rather short, repeated with minor variations, and highly ornamented with hammer-ons and pull-offs.

Tuning the Sapeh
The sapeh is tuned depending on the gauge of strings used, or how the instrument is constructed. Some instruments have

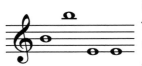

thumbtacks or small hooks to shorten the accompaniment strings, so that the same gauge can be used for all strings. Normally on a four-string sapeh, which is now the most common, the melody string is in unison with the first accompaniment string beside it. The next string would be tuned to either a third, fourth or fifth depending on the piece and wishes of the performer. The outside string is either tuned to an octave above either of the previous strings. The frets of the sapeh are only found under the melody string, are held in place with a malleable wax-like substance, and are movable to produce the two main modes: so, la, do, re, me and re, me, so, la, do. Often the frets must be slightly adjusted to fine tune the instrument, but caution is advised, as they can fall off and are easy to lose.

Ulu Malaam

26

Saz or Baglama - Turkey

The term saz means *instrument* in Persian and Turkish, and often refers to the instruments in the tanbur family that are now scattered throughout central Asia and the Middle East. Yet, recently the term saz has been used to describe the various sizes of Turkish long-necked lutes that are also called *baglama*. The Turkish saz has a pear shaped body traditionally carved from one piece of wood with a flat or slightly arched top, a long slender neck, gut frets and six or seven strings. It is a popular folk instrument traditionally used to accompany sung poetry, and now found in popular music as both a solo and ensemble instrument. The saz is fretted with gut frets that can be adjusted to play quartertones determined by the mode or *maqam* of the piece chosen.

Playing the Saz

Turkish music is complex, often changing maqams within a piece, and many maqams use quartertones. However, the saz can also be used in western scales and its deep rich sound can be very rewarding to play. The melody is usually played on the highest strings with the other strings as drones, but all the strings can be fretted as well. Three techniques are quite common and help to give the saz its characteristic sound. The first is the very rapid tremolo common to the Middle East (see *Rapid Picking*). The second is a rapid trilling between a note and the pitch on the adjacent higher fret even if it is not within the maqam or scale being played. The third is the percussive drumming on the soundboard with the fingers of the picking hand. The saz can be played either with the bare fingers or with a plastic or wooden plectrum.

Tuning the Saz

The most common tuning of the saz is G,d,a from the lowest to the highest gauge of string, although many variations exist. The strings are usually doubled but occasionally the highest string is tripled. Commonly the lowest strings are tuned in octaves or fourths, the middle strings are in unison and the highest strings are either in unison or in octaves. The tuning is often changed to suit either the singer's range or the maqam. Other possible saz tunings' include: E,d,a, F#,d,a, G,c,g, G,d,g, A,d,g, A,d,a, and A,E,a.

Ayazein — TRACK 19 — Traditional

(drone notes)

27

Seung - Thailand

The seung is a four-stringed lute of the Lanna people of Northern Thailand. The origins are unclear, but the seung, and its northeastern Thai cousin the *pin* are probably descended from the *krachappi*, a four-stringed classical northern Thai instrument that came from the Indian *Saraswati vina*. The seung is fretted diatonically and the strings are arranged in two doubled courses. The seung is used in small instrumental ensembles and to accompany singing. Recently, there has been a revival of Lanna music, and seung are increasingly becoming popular and easy to find.

Playing the Seung
The seung is held like a guitar and played with a soft plastic plectrum often made from a milk carton or a shirt stay. Seung music is characterized by a light lilting sound and a tremolo used in the place of long held notes.

Tuning the Seung
The strings are tuned in unison pairs of the tonic and either a fourth or fifth above on the lower strings, as the instrument is held. The tonic is usually a C or D but this is often adjusted to the singer.

Mae Sa

(repeat with variations)

Shamisen - Japan

The shamisen is the three-stringed lute of Japan, however it is more likely a member of the rebab family. The shamisen descended from the Chinese san xian, meaning *three strings,* which had three silk strings and a snakeskin top and back. However the modern shamisen uses nylon strings and the back and top are covered with cat skin. There are a number of different types of shamisen, each used in different forms of music and each varying in body size, length, neck width, plectrum and playing style. The most common shamisen on the market is the *Nagauta* style used to accompany vocal music, and most of these shamisen are collapsible to enable them to be carried in a small case. The most exciting shamisen style is *Tsugaru jamisen*, which has recently become extremely popular with Japanese youth, is marked by improvisational passages and many flamboyant techniques.

Playing the Shamisen

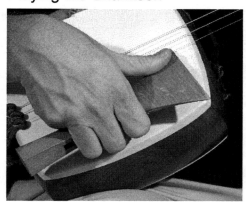

The shamisen is held with the neck to the left at a 45-degree angle, much like a classical guitar. The body rests balanced on the right leg so that the neck can stand free, and the right forearm sits on the top edge of the body to hold it in place. The left hand usually wears a small piece of knitted cloth that fits between the thumb and index finger to allow the hand to slide up and down the neck quickly. The shamisen uses a large plectrum called a *batchi* that is held in the right hand. The upward corner of the bachi picks the string in both the down and upstroke. It is possible to play a tremolo using the bachi, but extremely difficult. As the shamisen is fretless, large portamenti are common.

Tuning the Shamisen

There are three traditional tunings for the shamisen B,e,b, B,f♯,b, or B,e,a, that are usually adjusted up or down a tone to suit the range of a singer or ensemble. There are some contemporary variants, such as c,g,c', but these are composition specific.

Tsukubai

Sitar - India

The sitar is the North Indian long-necked lute with a gourd body, a hollow neck, raised curved frets and on some instruments a second gourd resonator. The sitar descended from the ancient three-stringed Persian *setar*, adding with time two drone strings, two punctuating strings known as *cikari*, and thirteen sympathetic strings. The sitar is a highly sophisticated instrument, performing long complex improvisational works formed around modal structures and strict rules of development called ragas. Popularized by Ravi Shankar and the Beatles in the 1960's, the sitar has become the most representative Indian instrument worldwide. It can be now found in many musical styles from rock to jazz, and there are sounds of the sitar on most commercial samplers.

Playing the Sitar

The sitar is a very complex instrument with a rich repertoire, and therefore learning to play traditional music is a daunting task. The serious student will take many years of study to even get to a moderate level. However the instrument can reward the tinkerer rather quickly with hours of pleasurable exploration, so it is worth taking up even casually. The sitar uses a wire pick called a *mizrab* that is placed over the index finger. The majority of the fretting is done on the outside string, which is often bent along the hoop frets towards the palm of the left hand to play not only quarter-tones but also short rapid ascending and descending progressions. The two inside *chikari* strings are used to provide a rhythmic counterpoint to the melody.

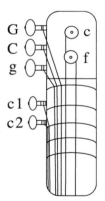

Ravi Shankar or Pancham-kharaj style

Tuning the Sitar

There are three main styles of sitar, each with its own string arrangement and tuning. The Vilayat Khan or *Gandhara-pancham* style has only six strings running across the main (larger) bridge, with a decorative top peg on the front of the instrument and tuned from the outside string in to f,C,E,g,c,c1. The Ravi Shankar or *Pancham-kharaj* style is the most popular and has seven strings tuned to f,C,G,c,g,c1,c2, three of which are brass or bronze strings. The older classical style is tuned to c,f,C,G,g,c1,c2. The sympathetic strings are tuned to the mode or raga that is being played, at the discretion of the performer. Tuning beads at the tail of the instrument aid in fine-tuning the main strings.

Saraswati

Traditional

Tambura - India

The tambura, also called a tampura, is a four-stringed Indian drone instrument commonly used behind all classical Indian performances. The tambura is at least four to five feet long with a large gourd body and a long hollow neck. Smaller, thinner instruments are being made to facilitate travel, but do not have as rich a sound. Since good quality instruments are getting increasingly hard to find, many musicians prefer using an electronic *shruti* box that approximates the sound of the tambura.

Playing the Tambura
Usually, the tambura is played with a slow steady pulse that may or may not be the same as the music. The tambura can be held with the neck pointing straight up or with the instrument lying on its side in the lap. The strings are plucked with only the very outside edges of the first two fingertips of the right hand, with the fingers held parallel to the strings. The touch should be very light almost as if the fingers were falling off the strings rather than plucking them. As the overtones peak substantially later than when plucked, it is important to listen carefully so as to properly time the plucking of the next string.

Tuning the Tambura
Traditionally, tamburas are tuned to the tonic on the inside string, an octave of the tonic on both the middle strings, and either the fourth or fifth on the outside string: C,g,g,G or C,c,c,F. However, as they are drone instruments, they can be tuned to a wide variety of tunings. Fine-tuning of the tambura is greatly facilitated with the tuning beads at the bottom of the strings. An important part of the tambura is the whine of the strings produced by the flat bridge called a *jawari*, and a small piece of thread placed between the string and the bridge. This thread is finely adjusted to produce a rich set of overtones with a long delay.

Tambura Drone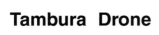

Tanbur - Uyghurstan, Western China

The tanbur is an extremely old Central Asian instrument dating back to the third century BC in Mesopotamia, usually distinguished by an extremely long neck and a small pear shaped body. Various forms of tanburs are found with a variety of names from eastern Europe to western China. Traditionally, tanburs have movable gut frets while more modern instruments have a set of wooden or steel frets. Uyghur tanburs more closely resemble European tanburs than those of Central Asia. They are distinguished by having five strings and an unusual fretting arrangement where some of the frets do not extend across the whole fret board. The Uyghur tanbur is used in small ensembles and to accompany singing. It has a fairly quiet and mellow tone.

Playing the Tanbur
The tanbur can be held like a guitar on the lap or up higher against the chest as is common in Central Asia. The latter seems an awkward position at first, but becomes comfortable with time. The tanbur is played with either a wooden or plastic plectrum to perform the characteristic rapid style of Central Asian picking. The two pairs of strings can be fretted, the inner strings with the thumb and the outer strings with the fingers. As the tanbur's neck is so long, it is usually played in its upper range, and so a couple of the lower frets are completely missing.

Tuning the Tanbur
Uyghur tanburs double the outside strings leaving a single center string, which is often used as a drone. There are a large number of tunings that vary with the musician and region, two common traditional tunings are gg,d,gg, dd,G,dd, and more contemporary tunings include gg,d,aa and aa,d aa.

Samani

32

Tar - Persia

The Persian tar is a plucked rebab with six strings arranged in double courses. The mulberry wood body is made in the shape of a figure eight and is covered with a thin skin made from a lamb's fetus. The tar has gut frets that can be adjusted to play quartertones commonly found in Persian modes. The strings are plucked with a thick brass plectrum called a *mizrab* that is coated on one end with beeswax to aid in gripping. The tar is considered a relatively new instrument in Persian standards, with historical references dating its origin from between five hundred to twelve hundred years ago. The Persian tar is similar to, although larger than, the Azerbaijan or Armenian tar.

Playing the Tar
Persian music is one of the most complex and sophisticated forms of music in the world, and as the tar is one of the most popular Persian instruments, its repertoire reflects the height of this musical form. Anyone taking up the tar has a wealth of knowledge ahead of them, and some big shoes to fill. Yet the tar is a wonderfully expressive instrument even for the novice or those not interested in tradition. Although the mizrab seems unwieldy at first, with practice it becomes a tool of great delicacy. Subtlety is the essence of the tar and accomplished performers distinguish themselves with delicate flourishes of grace notes and minute shifts of timing.

Tuning the Tar
There are seventy-two different tunings for the tar, depending on the modes, and expressions of the piece to be played. Many of these tunings require the open strings to be tuned in quartertones, and adjusting the frets to the modal arrangement needed. The most common tunings are cc1,gg,c1c1 or dd1, gg, c1c1.

Tar Melisma TRACK 25

Traditional

Ajaeng - Korea

The ajaeng is a Korean bowed zither with a wild earthy sound used in shamanistic rituals, in court and folk ensembles to accompany dance, and as an instrument of virtuosity. The eight thick silk strings pass over a very large curved main bridge, and then again over smaller movable bridges that are on the secondary top of the instrument.

Playing the Ajaeng

The ajaeng was traditionally played with a thin curved rosined stick, which produced a very rough sound, that has since been replaced by a violin bow. The instrument is placed on the floor and bowed from the right side next to the highest string. The player's left hand presses on the strings on the far side of the small bridges to raise the string to the next pitch and to produce the very deep form of tremolo characteristic to Korean music. The ajaeng is usually played in a pentatonic scale but Korean music also makes full use of ornamentations between two notes.

Tuning the Ajaeng

The ajaeng is tuned to a repeated tonic, fourth, fifth and tonic, starting from the lowest string. The smaller bridges on the top of the instrument are good for larger tuning adjustments, but there are also fine tuners on the underside of the instrument, which twist the string to tighten it. If a string breaks, there is an ample amount at the far end of the instrument that can be unraveled as a replacement. It is important that when retying the string, a proper amount of tension is applied, so the string can reach the proper pitch.

Seoraksan CD TRACK 26

Bro - Vietnam

The bro is the tube zither of the Ede people of the Central Highlands of Vietnam. It is a quiet, intimate instrument well suited to its traditional use of accompanying love songs. It is made from a thin piece of bamboo with a gourd attached a third the length of the instrument from one end. There are two strings that extend the length of the tube, only one of which passes over three to five small frets held in place with wax or pitch. The bro is played in a similar manner to the Malagasy *jejy vaotavo*, and both probably share a common origin in the fretted stick zithers of India.

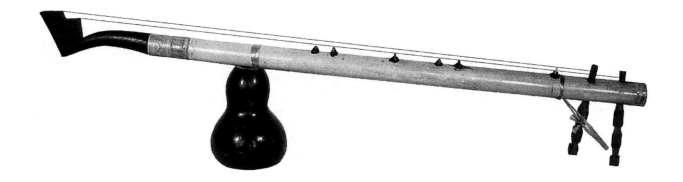

Playing the Bro
The bro is held horizontally between the thumb and fingers of both hands, with the thumbs on the top of the instrument. It is plucked by a flicking action of the right index finger on both strings, creating melody and a drone simultaneously, and fretted with the fingers of the left hand. The gourd is alternately moved back and fourth against the body to change the sound envelope, creating a *wah* effect.

Tuning the Bro
The bro is usually adjusted to a singer's voice and tuned to a fifth.

Cat Tien TRACK 27

(drone)

rit.

35

Chake - Thailand

The chake is a three-stringed zither found in central Thailand and Cambodia that used to be made in the shape of an alligator. Presently the chake has a long deep body that stands on small legs on the floor. The chake has raised frets, two thick nylon strings and one brass string that pass over a flattened metal bridge that gives the instrument a characteristic buzzing sound similar to the *sitar*. The chake is played with a large ivory or shark tooth plectrum that is tied to the index finger of the right hand. The chake is considered a part of the Thai classical or court tradition, and it is used as both a solo and an ensemble instrument. It has a seven-tone equidistant scale, and therefore does not include a perfect fifth or any other intervals found in the twelve-tone scale of the West.

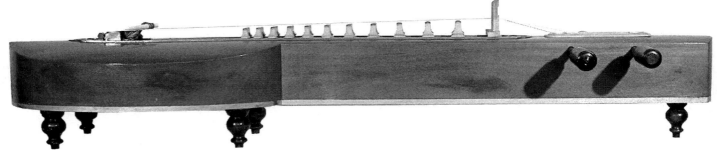

Playing the Chake
The chake pick is tied to the side of the index finger just below the first knuckle, and stabilized with the thumb while playing. The fingering is similar to that of the *Appalachian dulcimer*, however the chake is played in a pentatonic scale. Most of the melodies are played on the two nylon strings with the occasional foray into the bass string. Characteristic playing techniques are the tremolos that replace any held note, rapid successions of grace notes, and very fast hammer-ons.

Tuning the Chake
The chake is tuned to the orchestra or singer it is performing with. The brass string is tuned to the tonic, the middle string either a fourth or fifth above, and the high string an octave above the brass string. The strings should buzz or whine similar to a sitar, and this is created by a small piece of carefully adjusted wood placed under the string as it passes over the flat bridge.

Sai Yok

36

Citera - Hungary

The Hungarian citera is a member of the European lap zither family from which also hail the *German concert zither, autoharp*, and *Appalachian dulcimer*. The citera has four main strings that can be fretted plus a number of drone and incidental strings. The citera's fretboard, located on top of the soundbox, has diatonic spaced frets under the first two strings (similar to the Appalachian dulcimer). The rest of the frets under the next two strings provide a fully chromatic scale through a somewhat awkward fingering. The citera does not have a back and is played on a table for amplification. Traditionally the citera is played accompanied by a four string cello-shaped instrument known as a *cordon* that is struck with a stick as a percussive background.

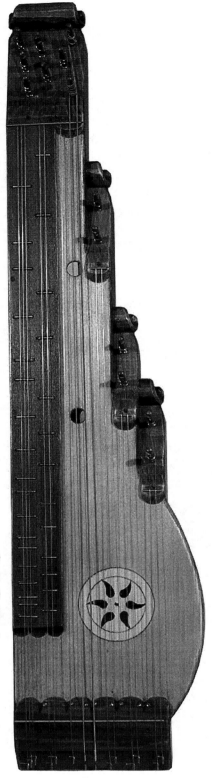

Playing the Citera
The citera is placed on a table with the fretboard closest to the performer. The right hand plucks and strums with a plastic plectrum while the left hand frets the strings. The melody is primarily played on the first three unison strings and only use the next two unison strings when accidentals are required, otherwise they are used as drones. The rest of the strings are plucked randomly for expression. Citera are often played with a great amount of speed and power.

Tuning the Citera
Usually one citera is required for each key the performer wishes to play in, so citera players often have three or four instruments with them in order to change keys. All the strings over the fret board are tuned in unison to allow the player to play chromatically when desired. The rest of the strings are usually tuned to tonics and fifths, although other pitches such as thirds or sevenths are possible.

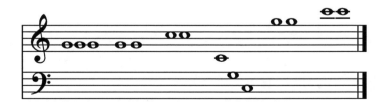

Beesteledik

37

Dan Bau - Vietnam

The dan bau is a one-string zither from Vietnam that plays in harmonics. *Dan* in Vietnamese signifies an instrument, so often the instrument is just referred to as a *bau*. Some scholars believe that the dan bau is related to the Thai *pin pia*, while others believe that it is a uniquely Vietnamese instrument. The dan bau has a narrow rectangular box for a body with a single string angling up from the right side to attach to the *vòi dàn,* the thin stick usually made of water buffalo horn at the other end of the instrument. Acoustic dan bau are extremely quiet and now rare, having been replaced by electric bau. Dan bau are native to North Vietnam, as well as the Jing people of Guangxi province in southern China where some bau are made with a bamboo body.

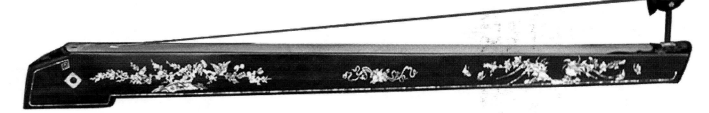

Playing the Dan Bau
Playing the bau is a bit of a challenge at first as it is played almost exclusively in harmonics. It is helpful to mark the positions of the harmonics on the body of the instrument with a piece of tape. Holding a long wooden plectrum shaped like a toothpick between the thumb and index finger of the right hand, the player touches the

harmonic point with the side of the palm while plucking the string, lifting the hand quickly to allow the harmonic to ring. The harmonics played are from the centre of the string towards the vòi dàn, and the vòi dàn is then pressed or pulled horizontally to raise or lower the pitch, as well as to create vibrato and bent notes. The art of the dan bau is found in the technique of the vòi dàn.

Tuning the Dan Bau
The bau traditionally accompanies singing, so the instrument is usually tuned to the voice. On the modern electric bau, a guitar tuner has replaced the traditional wooden tuning peg, so changing pitch is very quick and easy, although it is most commonly tuned to C.

Vong Co   TRACK 30   Traditional

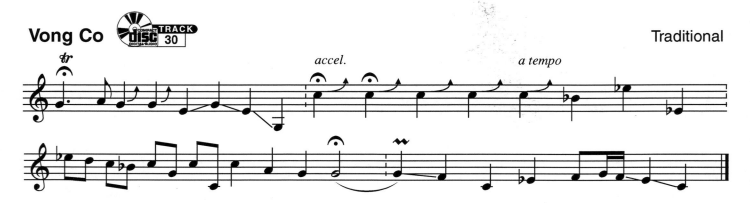

Dan Tranh - Vietnam

The Vietnamese dan tranh is the smallest version of the Asian long zither family. It has a sharply convex top, sixteen metal strings, and tuning pegs inserted directly into the top of the instrument. Much quieter than other long zithers, the dan tranh is used as a solo instrument, to accompany singers, and in small ensembles.

Playing the Dan Tranh
Playing the dan tranh is similar to playing the Chinese zheng, but because the strings are very thin it demands a very light touch. Metal, plastic, or bone fingerpicks are used on the thumb and first two fingers of the right hand, and resemble the wrap around style of banjo or guitar picks, which bend over the front of the finger. The light and subtle left-hand technique on the left side of the bridge defines the dan tranh's music.

Tuning the Dan Tranh
The dan tranh is tuned in a variety of modes based on the basic pentatonic scale do re me so la, repeated in three octaves. Traditional Vietnamese music does not always follow Western temperament and there are a number of modes that have raised fourths or flat sevenths. Large tuning changes are made by using the tuning pegs, while fine-tuning is achieved by moving the bridges.

Halong

(bend & release)

39

Ichigenkin and Nigenkin - Japan

The ichigenkin and nigenkin are very rare one and two-string Japanese zithers respectively. The ichigenkin has a simple design with only one silk string, a tuning peg, a bridge, and a curved plank of palownia wood for a body. Lacking a sound box or resonator, the sound of the ichigenkin is very subtle, and it was often used as an instrument of contemplation, or to accompany sung poetry. The ichigenkin's simplicity and beauty made it an ideal expression of Zen, used through the centuries by samurai, literati, and Buddhist monks. The nigenkin is a descendant of the ichigenkin and has a slightly larger body with a flat top and sides. The nigenkin's two strings pass over bridges at both ends of the instrument, with the bridge at the head of the instrument amplifying the overtones on the side of the string not plucked. The nigenkin is used to accompany secular songs. Both instruments have small ivory or jeweled note markers that run beside the string.

Playing the Ichigenkin and Nigenkin
Both instruments are usually played on a table or a small stand. The plectrum is a rather bulky tube of ivory, plastic, or bamboo that fits over the top of the index finger and is cut at an oblique angle to match the angle of the fingertip. To strike the string, the right hand pivots on the first knuckle of the little finger with all the fingers immobile and only flexing the wrist. The string is fretted using a *rokan*, a tube of the same thickness as the plectrum but longer that fits over the second finger of the left hand. The rokan lightly slides along the string like on a slide guitar, and does not push the string into the body. Both strings of the nigenkin are plucked as a single string, though occasionally they may be plucked individually for special effect. Portamenti are very important to both instruments, sometimes even used without plucking.

Tuning the Ichigenkin and Nigenkin
Both the ichigenkin and nigenkin are simply tuned to the player's voice, to accompanying instruments, or to an appropriate tension for the gauge of string, most often in the region of C or D. The nigenkin's strings are tuned in unison. The ichigenkin usually uses a raw silk string whereas the nigenkin uses much thinner nylon strings.

Saihoji

40

Kacapi and Siter - Indonesia

Indonesian zithers come in a number of shapes and sizes, but are basically quite similar. Kacapi are mid-size box zithers from West Java. The sound of the kacapi has become quite well known around the world due to the popularity of kacapi suling music, arguably one of the most beautiful styles of Sundanese music. The siter is a sister instrument of similar size with a slightly different shape that is often exchangeable with the kacapi.

Playing the Kacapi
The player usually sits either to the right side of the instrument or at the end of the instrument, plucking the strings with the thumb and index fingers of both hands. Sometimes the hands play independent interlocking parts, while at other times they may play passages in octaves. Some contemporary works have demanded the kacapi perform very intricate and rapid solos, and virtuosic techniques for this instrument are still being developed.

Tuning the Kacapi
Kacapi or siters are tuned to either an accompanying suling flute or gamelan orchestra, with the two main scales being pelog, an anhemitonic pentatonic scale of so la, do, re, fa, and slendro, a hemitonic pentatonic scale of so, ti, do, re, fa. It should be noted that Indonesian temperament is different from western temperament, so intervals may vary from what the western ear is used to hearing. Large tuning changes are made by using the tuning pegs, while fine-tuning is achieved by moving the bridges.

Kawah Putih TRACK 33

Kayagum - Korea

The kayagum is the twelve-string long zither of Korea. There are two forms of kayagum, a larger court version that has two large wings or horns at the end, and the smaller sanjo version used as an instrument of virtuosity, to accompany singing, and in small ensembles. The kayagum has silk strings that are attached to the instrument in such a way that if a string is broken, a substantial length of string is still available to be unfurled at the far end of the instrument to replace it. The kayagum was fashioned after the ancient Chinese *zheng* and it still bears a striking resemblance to early zheng.

Playing the Kayagum
The kayagum is plucked with the fingers of the right hand on the right side of the bridges, while the left hand presses the string on the other side of the bridges to create bent notes and vibrato. The left-hand techniques resemble that of the *zheng* or *koto* but even more expressive. There are a number of distinct right hand techniques exclusive to the kayagum, including the index finger alternating between plucking the string and flicking it with the nail with force by first catching the side of the finger with the thumb and applying pressure to the finger before its release, much like flicking a piece of dust. A more elaborate version is one of the most fundamental kayagum techniques. The index fingers plucks, then the second finger flicks the string followed by the index finger flicking. The second finger is tucked behind the first finger to provide force in the same manner the first tucks behind the thumb. This technique is done extremely quickly and repeated continuously to provide a version of a roll. Two styles of muting are common either by dampening a string with an adjacent finger immediately after it is plucked, or by dampening a string with the base of the hand while it is plucked. Other right hand techniques include glissandi and the alteration of the thumb and forefinger, both common to the koto and zheng as well.

Step 1.
While resting the thumb on the string above the one you want to play, pluck the desired string with the index finger.

Step 2.
Quickly tuck the index finger behind the thumb and then the second finger behind the index finger. Putting pressure on the second finger, release it to strike the same string as above with force.

Step 3.
Strike the string with the index finger in the same manner as with the second finger. Then repeat all three steps.

Tuning the Kayagum
The kayagum is tuned to a pentatonic scale with a small variation at the lower end. Although a typical traditional tuning is F,Bb,c,f,g,bb,c1,d1,f1,g1,bb1, c2, the scale can be changed to suit the vocal range of a singer, and there are now many contemporary tunings as well. Normally, tuning is achieved by moving the bridges and fine-tuning is accomplished by turning the small knobs attached to each string on the underside of the top end of the instrument. Large tuning changes are achieved by loosening the rope attached to the string at the base of the instrument, and then tightening it again with greater tension.

Soraksan

Koto - Japan

The Japanese koto, a descendant of the Chinese zheng, is perhaps the most well known member of the Asian long zither family. The koto is over six feet or two meters in length and is made from palownia wood. The modern koto has thirteen nylon strings stretched over plastic or ivory bridges and is played with three plastic or ivory picks, both as a solo instrument and in ensembles.

Playing the Koto
There are two major schools of koto with different shaped picks known as *tsume*, and both schools wear tsume on the thumb and first two fingers. The *Yamada* tsume are rounded on the end with the tips used to pluck the strings. *Ikuta* tsume are flat at the end with sharp corners, using the left corner of the thumb pick and the right corner of the finger picks to pluck the strings. Traditionally tsume were made of ivory, but now plastic is more common. Tsume are fastened into a small ring of leather using smashed cooked rice as glue. The tsume are positioned so that the pick is on the inside of the fingers and a small amount of egg white applied to the finger prevents the leather ring from slipping.

To play the koto, the performer sits to the right closest to the thinnest string, with the bridges running diagonally to the left away from them. The left hand pushes the string about one hand length to the left side of the bridges to create a vibrato or to raise the pitch of the string by up to a third. The right hand plucks to the right of the bridges with the thumb and first two fingers. Typical gestures include playing in octaves, tremolo played with the thumb, large glissandi, and striking the two lowest strings at the same time.

Tuning the koto
The koto is traditionally tuned pentatonically, although there are now many modern tunings. The most common tuning is called *Hira-joshi* G, A, Bb, d, eb (la, ti, do, mi, fa) from low to high. It is important to note that the lowest pitch on the instrument is often not found on the lowest string, but the second to lowest string. The lowest string can be tuned a fifth higher than the lowest pitch. Tuning is achieved by moving the bridges. It is better to leave replacing a string for the experienced or adventurous, as strings are tightened to a very taut uniform tension that requires the use of the feet against the tail of the instrument and a piece of rubber to protect the hand while pulling and tying at the same time.

Tajima TRACK 35

Lutong - Malaysia

The lutong is a four to six string bamboo tube zither found in the Malaysian province of Sarawak on the island of Borneo. It is almost identical to the tube zithers found throughout Sabah, Indonesia and the Philippines. In Sarawak, the lutong was a woman's instrument, often traditionally played at the head of a woman's dance celebrating a successful headhunting raid. The strings are made from the peel of the bamboo, which are pulled up and prevented from totally being pulled apart from the body by bindings on either end. Small pieces of bamboo are used as bridges under the two sides of the string to add tension and can be adjusted for tuning.

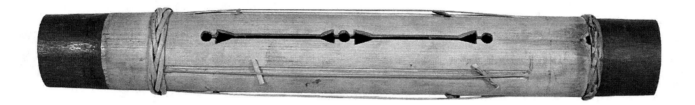

Playing the Lutong
The lutong is held forward away from the body so that one end rests on the leg if sitting, or stomach if standing. The thumbs, and the first one or two fingers of both hands, pluck the strings while the other fingers may be used to brace the instrument. Often strings may be muted very quickly to produce a staccato note. This is accomplished with either the tip of the finger that plucks that string or any finger joint closest to the string. The lutong is very quiet, so amplification may be needed to play with other instruments.

Tuning the Lutong
Usually bamboo zithers are tuned to the pitches of an anhemitonic pentatonic scale of la, do, re, mi, so. The small bridges at either end of the string are adjusted to tune the string, however, if the string is too high or too low, then larger or smaller bridges are used as appropriate. It is very important that the string is not completely pulled off the body of the instrument, as it will no longer function.

Long San

45

Mvet - Cameroon

The mvet is an African stick zither found in a variety of similar forms in a number of regions. Traditionally, the mvet is made from a raffia stalk approximately one meter long, with four or more strings running across a central bridge and attached to both ends of the body. There are three gourd resonators, one at each end and another in the middle. The mvet is used to accompany epic poems and the sung history of the peoples who play it. Mvet players are highly honoured and go through intensive training.

Playing the Mvet
The mvet is held with the central gourd against the stomach and at a forty-five degree angle so that the left hand reaches underneath to pluck the strings and the right hand reaches over the top of the body. The instrument can be held with either the thumbs or the forearms depending on the size of the instrument. Often rapid alternating lines with compound rhythms are used, requiring great skill from the performer.

Tuning the Mvet
Mvet are tuned to a diatonic scale, alternating between the two sides of the bridge to facilitate playing. While modern mvet have tuning pegs, the strings on older mvet are attached directly to the body and are adjusted by moving this attachment along the body. Mvet are often tuned to a singer's voice.

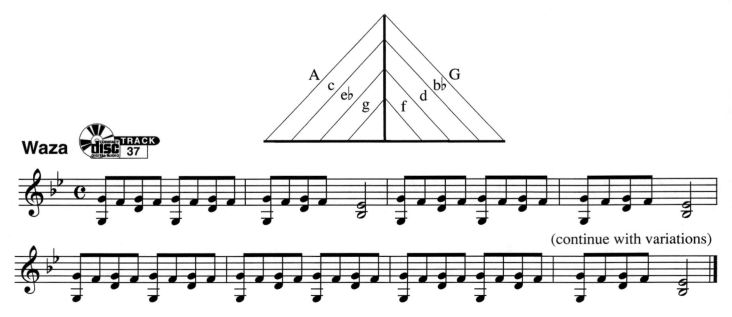

Waza

(continue with variations)

Pin Pia - Thailand

The pin pia is a stick zither of the Lanna people of the Chiang Mai region of Northern Thailand. The origin of the pin pia is from the Indian *alapini vina*, which is now extinct, but still can be seen pictured on a mid seventh century temple carving at *Bala-Brahma* temple in Alampur, Andhra Pradesh, India. The pin pia has two strings, although earlier versions may have had only one string like its Cambodian cousin, the *kse diev.* Modern pin pia can also be found with three or four strings, but all function on the same principle of one melody string played in harmonics and fretted, with the accompaniment strings plucked open.

Playing the Pin Pia

Playing the pin pia is a bit challenging. The right hand must pluck the melody string with the third finger, while touching the same string at harmonic points with the first joint of the first finger. Three harmonics are usually used, the first found half way along the string, the second found another half the remaining length, and the third again half the remaining length. Accomplished players with good instruments can use more harmonic points. The left hand alternately plucks the accompaniment strings and frets the melody string against the body, however the position of the harmonic must be adjusted slightly when the melody string is fretted. The typical Thai style does not slide into or out of notes when fretting with the left hand, although it is common on other stick zithers in this family. Pin pia are often played in pairs or in a small ensembles with a seung.

Hold the pin pia between the left thumb and fingers so the fingers are free to fret the first string, and pluck the other strings.

Touch the first string at harmonic points with the knuckle at the base of the right index finger and pluck the same string with the third finger.

Tuning the Pin Pia

The outer accompaniment string on the two-stringed pin pia is tuned a fourth higher than the inner melody string. The three-stringed pin pia is tuned to tonic, major or minor third, and a fourth. The four-stringed pin pia is tuned the same as the three string but adds a whole tone below the tonic on the last string.

Noi Dok Mai TRACK 38

47

Santur - Iran (Persia)

The Persian santur is a percussive box zither, commonly referred to as a hammer dulcimer. Originating in Assyria or Chaldea as early as sixth century BC, the santur is the parent of both the hammer dulcimer family and the piano. The santur comes in different sizes with different numbers of strings. Traditionally santur have two rows of bridges, called *kharak,* arranged so that all the strings on the santur can be played except those to the right of the right row of bridges. The santur is used for both classical and popular music.

Playing the Santur
The santur is played with very light hammers that partially wrap around the in index finger of each hand. The santur is hammered rapidly, making great use of tremolo created with the wrists and not by bouncing the hammers on the strings. Santur music is very expressive with a much greater range of dynamics than other forms of hammer dulcimers.

Tuning the Santur
The santur is usually tuned to the scale or mode that the piece is in. As in any hammer dulcimer, it is important to position the bridges so that the notes on either side of it are in tune with each other. Unlike other hammer dulcimers, the pitches on either side of the left kharak are tuned an octave apart.

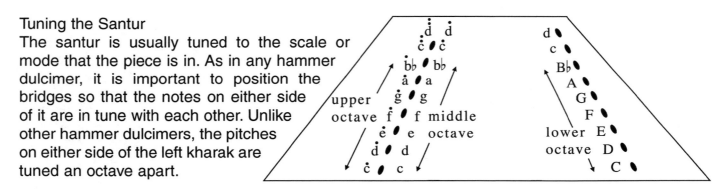

Alborz

Toba or Hanhye - Benin

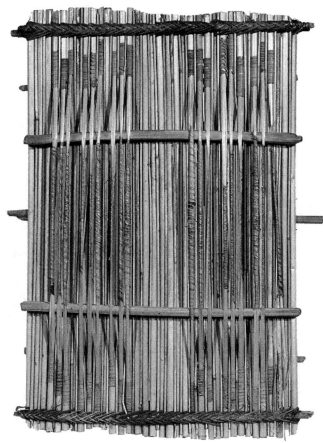

The toba is a raft zither of the Mahi people of Benin, used to accompany songs and occasionally used in small ensembles. It resembles a small mat or raft as it is constructed of thin sticks or reed tied to two cross bars. The skins of some of these reeds are pulled up to become strings and bound with fibre to increase the thickness of the string to get lower pitches. Two wide bridges are inserted at each end of the instrument under all the strings. As the instrument is not loud, it is often played over a gourd, clay pot or bucket to add resonance. Often there are small metal jingles attached in some manner to provide an additional percussive element.

Playing the Toba
The toba is held by its sides between the hands and plucked with the thumbs. Single strings or groups of strings are played in rhythmic patterns. Caution must be taken not to play the strings with too much force, they are fragile and once broken they are almost impossible to fix.

Tuning the Toba
Each string on the toba is bound to a stick so the peel won't completely detach. These bindings are movable, and subtle adjustments can make a substantial change to the pitch of the string. It is often tuned in chords or to emphasize rhythmic-melodic phrases. The toba is often tuned to an ensemble or at the discretion of the performer.

Oueme TRACK 40

(Repeat selected rhythms with variations)

Hand = R   L   R   L R L

49

Valiha - Madagascar

The valiha is the tube zither of Madagascar, with roots in the tube zithers of eastern Borneo. Originally made from a piece of bamboo with the strings pulled up from the skin, modern valiha come in many shapes and sizes from meter long bamboo tubes with metal strings to large box-like instruments with metal strings on both sizes. The number of strings varies with the style of instrument and from which region of Madagascar they originate. Almost exclusively played by men, valiha were traditionally used in ritual ceremonies. Now they are used in a number of musical styles and are popular as an entertainment instrument internationally. Although traditional instruments are still on the market, modern valiha are becoming much more common.

Playing the Valiha
The most common valiha is the tube zither type, which only has strings at one end. The end without strings is tucked under the right arm and held in place with the upper arm with the lowest string facing the performer. The strings are then plucked with the thumbs and first two fingers of both hands, with advance players using all their fingers. If sitting, one end of the valiha can be rested on the floor.

Tuning the Valiha
The valiha is usually tuned to a diatonic scale with the centre string as the tonic and alternating between sides to facilitate ease of performance. As the strings are usually fixed, small bridges of gourd or bamboo are placed under the strings at each end, and are moved to adjust the tuning.

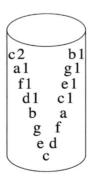

c2   b1
  a1   g1
    f1   e1
    d1   c1
      b   a
       g f
        e d
          c

Lokobe CD TRACK 41

(repeat with variations)

50

Zheng - China

The Chinese zheng is the parent instrument of the Asian long zither family, invented during the Warring States Period (475-221 BC) or earlier. The zheng was an important part of Chinese history as a court and folk instrument, and many centuries old stylistic schools of playing are still in existence today. Older and regional zhengs are usually about four feet long, with thirteen to sixteen steel strings. The standard zheng now is about five feet, or one and a half meters, in length and has twenty-one strings made of steel, or metal wound with nylon. There are a few rare modern zhengs with more strings and different shapes.

Playing the Zheng
Traditionally zheng were played with the fingernails, but now zheng players wear four picks made of plastic or tortoise shell attached to the inside of the thumb and fingers with medical or sports tape, with one large hooked pick for the thumb and three straight picks for the fingers. The player sits to the right side of the zheng close to the high string, with the bridges angling away diagonally to the left. The left hand often depresses a string about one finger length to the left side of the bridge to create a vibrato or to raise the pitch of the string by up to a minor third. The right hand plucks the strings with the thumb and fingers on the right side of the bridges. Typical techniques include: playing in octaves; a tremolo played with the thumb or index finger only (called *yao* in Chinese); large glissandi from top to bottom or bottom to top (*hua* in Chinese); and a repetitive finger pattern of thumb, second finger, thumb, first finger on adjacent strings.

Taping on the
fingerpicks
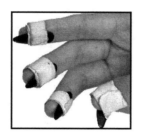

Hand position
on the strings
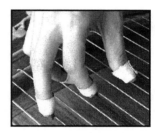

Tuning the Zheng
The zheng is often tuned to a D pentatonic scale over four octaves: D, E, F♯, A, B (do, re, mi, so, la) from low to high. Most modern zheng are strung with four white strings and a green string per octave, with the green string tuned to A. The strings can be adjusted by moving the bridge on top of the sound-board to make fine adjustments. Larger tuning adjustments are usually made by turning the tuning pegs found in the box on the large end of the instrument.

Spring Flower in the Moonlight

51

Dizi - China

The dizi is the transverse (side-blown) flute of China, traditionally made from bamboo. The dizi comes in two sizes, the smaller northern *bangdi*, and the larger southern *qudi* with a richer tone. The dizi is distinguished by a hole placed between the aperture and the finger-holes that is covered by a very fragile paper-like-fiber that comes from the inner lining of a type of reed or bamboo. This fiber, called *di mo*, vibrates when the instrument is played, giving the dizi its characteristic tone. The dizi is approximately a thousand years old, and probably developed from the six thousand year-old *chi*, a Chinese transverse flute without the di mo. The dizi is now the main flute of China.

Adjusting the Dizi
Before playing the dizi, the di mo must be properly applied and adjusted. Although the flute will work by covering this hole with tape, it will not sound like a dizi. Di mo is inexpensive and can be bought online. It comes in a small package and is very fragile. Take out a single sheet and cut a piece so that it will fit easily over the hole with a good size border. Be careful to cut the piece so that the grain of the di mo is at right angles to the flute. Roll the di mo into a ball between your fingers for a couple of minutes and then carefully unravel it

until it is flat. Cut a small piece of fresh garlic and put a small amount of garlic juice around the hole, being careful not to get it in the hole. Place the di mo over the hole with the grain running at a right angle to the flute, the garlic juice should hold it in place, but a small amount of moisture on the edges of the di mo will assist in adjusting it. Do not pull the di mo very tight, instead, allow for a slight slackness. If adjusted properly the flute should sound with a slight buzzing of the di mo, if it is too loose the flute won't sound, but if too tight the di mo will not sound. When the di mo is too tight breathe moist air onto it, and when too loose put the di mo next to your cheek to warm it up. Adjusting the di mo is an art in itself and takes time to learn and perfect.

Playing the Dizi
The dizi is held in the same fashion as the western orchestral flute, and played with a good tight embouchure. It is said that a good dizi player can play facing the wind, which is a very challenging task for any flute player. There are slight differences in the performance between the qudi and bangdi. Typically, the qudi is not tongued, instead, notes and rhythm are emphasized by a pronounced striking of the fingerholes with the fingers just before sounding the note. Bangdi technique emphasizes bent notes and large rapid glissandi.

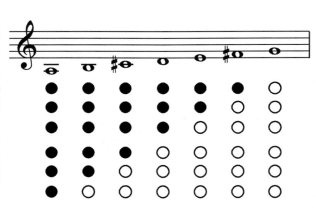

Yu Zhou Chang Wan 🎵 TRACK 43

Traditional

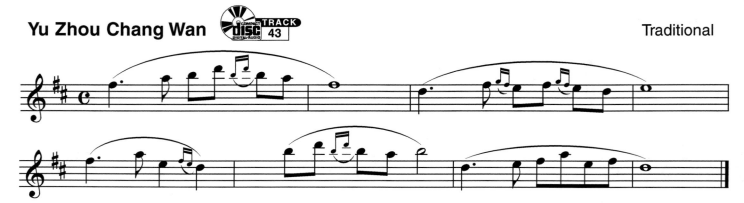

Fujara - Slovakia

The fujara is a very long double-channeled duct flute from Slovakia that has become quite popular throughout Europe and is gaining popularity in North America for its distinctive sound. The longest pipe can reach up to six feet or 2 meters in length and has three finger holes. A smaller pipe that contains the mouthpiece is connected to the top of the long pipe. Many modern instruments are made in a number of pieces so the instrument can be dismantled for travel, yet traditional instruments still seem to sound better.

Playing the Fujara
The fujara is mostly played in overtones, and this is accomplished by over-blowing, but it takes practice to obtain the desired accuracy. The fingering is unusual, often varying with the performer and the instrument, as the finger holes on fujara are spread far apart. A common way of holding the instrument is with the left thumb and forefinger, with the left third finger closing the top hole. The right thumb closes the center hole and the third finger the bottom hole. At first it may seem awkward, but it soon makes sense.

Fingering Chart

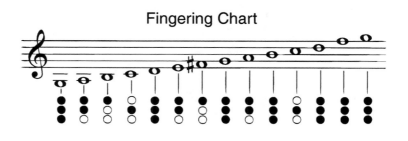

Nizke Tatry TRACK 44   Traditional

53

Maceno, Mohoceno, or Moseno - Bolivia

The maceño is a duct flute played by various indigenous peoples of Bolivia. It has two parts, a thin bamboo pipe housing the aperture, which runs one half the length of the main larger bamboo pipe that forms the main body and contains both the fipple and fingerholes. Traditionally these instruments are unpainted and quite large with a deep tone, but the tourist industry has created much smaller instrument usually painted with very bright colours. Maceño were traditionally played in ensembles with the melody hocketed between the musicians. Contemporary styles have instruments playing together in parallel thirds, fourths or fifths. There are five main fingerholes on the maceño and one extra hole that is often not used.

Playing the Maceño
The maceño is held like a traditional transverse flute, except the mouth fully covers and blows into the hole on the thin pipe. The first two fingers of the left hand cover the top two fingerholes and the first three right fingers the bottom three, there is an extra hole to the side that the right little finger could play if desired. The maceño is usually played in pentatonic scales and often jumps between octaves.

Fingering Chart

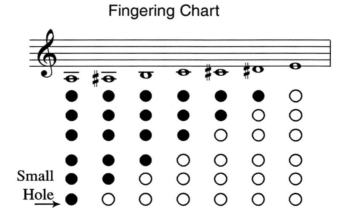

Kaa Iya Luna TRACK 45

54

Ney or Nay - Middle East

Ney are the oblique rim blown flutes of the Middle East and Arabic world, found in a number of different types, sizes and playing styles. It functions as the primary flute of the Middle East used in almost all forms of music. Ney were found in Egypt over five thousand years ago and have not changed much since. Ney are usually made from a type of hollow reed (the term ney means reed) with a number of holes on the front and usually one hole on the back. The Egyptian ney has no mouthpiece, instead, the top is sanded to sharpen the edge for clarity of performance. The Persian ney has a brass, bone, horn or ivory mouthpiece that is simply an extension of the reed with a sharp edge. The Turkish ney has a mushroom shaped mouthpiece made from wood, bone or horn.

Turkish

Playing the Ney

Producing a tone on a ney can take some time. The instrument is held at a slight oblique angle with the end slightly forward. Arabic (Egyptian, Turkish) ney are posi-

tioned with the top against the lips, the Persian ney are positioned against the teeth. In both cases a thin stream of air is directed towards the left edge of the top rim. The lips fill most of the rest of the aperture of the Arabic ney and are closed, except for a pin-prick stream of air. When learning to blow, less air is far more successful

than more air. The Persian ney is much more difficult and usually requires the player to have a gap between their front teeth to position the mouthpiece between. Some

players actually have their teeth filed to produce a gap. Usually the left side of the rim is positioned in the gap, with the rest of the rim completely under the upper lip. Air is channeled just behind the teeth. It is possible to play the Persian ney without a gap in the teeth by using the tongue to channel the air but

this technique is limited. Both styles can produce clear and very airy sounds by adjusting the position of the flute, and by using the tongue on the Persian ney. Both styles use quarter-tones which can be produced by partial fingering of the holes as well as slightly altering the position of the flute from center to side.

Persian

Egyptian

Fingering Chart

Tilt Head

Zaranik

Ohe Hano Ihu - Hawaii

The ohe hano ihu is the three-holed nose flute of Hawaii. Constructed of thick walled bamboo, this nose flute has a wide diameter but is quite short in length. Only capable of one octave, it is a remarkable beautiful instrument in the hands of a good player. Traditionally, it was used between lovers, and to relax someone getting a tattoo. The ohe hano ihu almost went extinct, but it has recently been undergoing a revival and many professional musicians are taking an interest in the instrument again. It is one of the few nose flutes that can be purchased easily online. Unfortunately, traditional music for this instrument has been lost, so Hawaiian musicians are creating new music for it. Some people mistake the ohe hano ihu for a lip flute because the aperture is placed in a similar position to a lip flute.

Playing the Ohe Hano Ihu

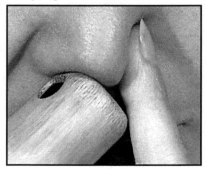

The ohe hano ihu is played by resting the end of the flute just inside and against the left side of the right nostril. The flute is then angled down forty-five degrees and slightly away form the body so that the aperture is very close to the right side of the nostril. The left hand holds the top of the flute against the nostril while plugging the left nostril at the same time. Vibrato is added by fluttering the diaphram.

Fingering Chart

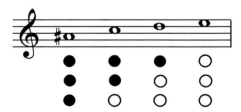

Halawa

56

Plains Flute - North America

The plains flute is a courting instrument of many of the native peoples of the central plains of North America. Although North American native peoples have had a wide variety of flutes and whistles for thousands of years, this rather recent instrument has gained great popularity and is used by both native and non-native people. The history of this instrument is a bit vague, yet it is known to have spread throughout the native communities in the mid-nineteenth century, and then again throughout the international community in the late twentieth century. This flute was primarily used by young men for courting, but as this tradition has died out in many communities, there is very little traditional music still being played. Most performers are either writing new music or are adapting other traditional songs.

Playing the Plains Flute
An important part in playing this instrument is to have the block over the fipple properly adjusted. If the block covers the hole completely or is too far back along the hole then the flute will not sound. It is important to adjust the block by moving it back and forth in very small increments to find the most responsive point and then secure it there tightly. This is usually done by tightening the leather strip that holds it in place. If the leather keeps stretching and will not stay tight, wet the leather first and then tie it very firmly. The leather will tighten as it dries. The Plains flute is restricted to a single octave and most modern instruments are made to play a pentatonic scale, although the tuning can vary radically with older instruments. It is played by blowing lightly into the end and moving the fingers progressively off the holes. Most plains flutes have a soft plaintive tone.

Fingering Chart

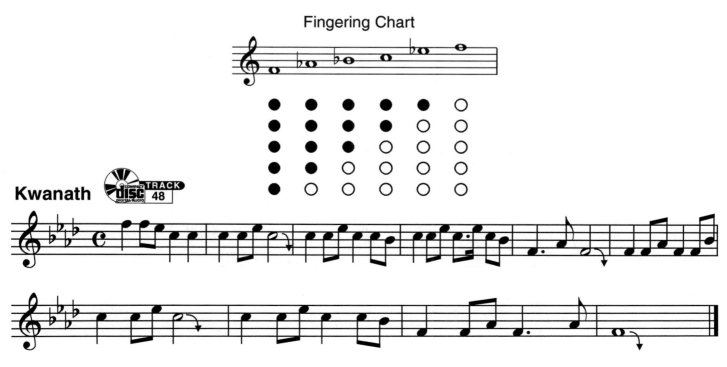

Kwanath

57

Quena - South America

The quena is the end-blown notch flute of the Andes, found in a variety of sizes and styles. With a history of almost three thousand years, the quena has been made from bamboo, wood, clay or bone. Quena come with differing number of fingerholes, but they all bear the characteristic notch at the top of the instrument, and are completely hollow. Well made quena can reach two or more octaves. Quena have gained international popularity and have gone from playing pentatonic to diatonic and even chromatic scales in the hands of advanced players. There are now modern quena with mechanical keys.

Playing the Quena
The quena is held at a forty-five degree angle directly in front of the body with the player's bottom lip partially resting inside the aperture. The top lip protrudes slightly to direct the air down towards the notch. A characteristic technique on the quena is the rapid and almost constant deep fluttering of the diaphragm to create a strong vibrato. Advanced players can also quarter hole and half hole the quena to play other pitches. Often quena are played in parallel thirds, fourths or fifths by two or more players.

Fingering Chart

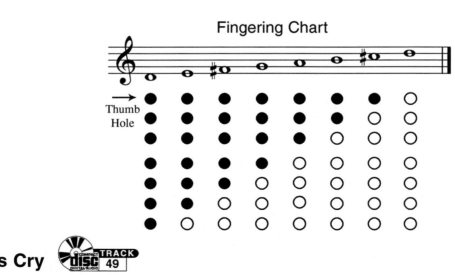

Inca's Cry TRACK 49

Traditional

58

Selingut - Malaysia

The selingut is the nose flute of the Kenyah and Kayan peoples of Borneo. There are a number of other nose flutes in the region that are played similar to, and in the same manner as, the selingut, including the Kejamin *selingup*, the Semang *pensol* and the Philippine *tongali*. Depending on the local customs, nose flutes could be traditionally used between lovers or to appease departed spirits. These nose flutes have a very beautiful sound that, although soft, travels very well in the jungle night air. These flutes are easily distinguished by the fact that they are all made from a narrow section of thin bamboo, and that the closed end of the flute has a slightly off center aperture carved into it. Fingerholes on the selingut vary from three to five.

Playing the Selingut

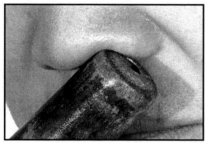

The selingut is played by placing the end of the flute into the left nostril so that there is a small gap between the left side of the left nostril and the end of the flute. The flute is held at an oblique angle crossing the body. The lower notes are usually very quiet and take a very small subtle amount of air to sound. Selingut are capable of at least two octaves through overblowing, but the tone remains clear, unlike the cracked tone of their Philippine relatives. Sometimes players will block the empty nostril with paper or cotton, although advance players can control the air so that it only comes out of one nostril. Selingut are played in pentatonic scales.

Fingering Chart

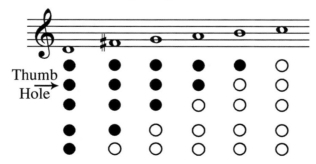

Laput Petang TRACK 50

(continue with variations)

Seljefløyte - Norway

The seljefløyte is the Norwegian name for a willow flute, called *sälgflöjt* in Sweden, and by a number of other names throughout Europe. It is an end-blown fipple flute that usually contains no fingerholes. These were traditionally made once a year when the willow bark was pliable enough to strip from the tree. The bark was rolled into the flute and the fipple made from cutting a slot into it and inserting a wooden or cork plug. It was used for personal entertainment and to accompany folk songs. In the West this type of flute are commonly called octave flutes or willow flutes, and are made with plastic pipe covered by bark.

Playing the Seljefløyte

The seljefløyte is held in one hand only, at the end of the flute, so that the index finger can completely close the end. The mouthpiece is placed in the mouth and gently blown to get the first note. The second is created buy simply closing off the end of the flute. The third note is then produced with an open end and increasing the wind pressure to over-blow slightly, and the fourth note by closing the end at this pressure. This process is repeated to get quite an impressive range of tones. Basically, the seljefløyte is played by switching back and forth between two harmonic series, that of the open pipe and that of the closed pipe. Vibrato and bent notes are achieved by subtle movements of the finger over the end of the flute.

Stabbursdalen

Shakuhachi - Japan

The shakuhachi is the Japanese end-blown notch flute found in many forms of music in Japan. The shakuhachi descended from the Chinese *xiao*, and is made from a thick piece of bamboo usually with part of the root still attached, providing a slight bell. The shakuhachi has four fingerholes in front and one in the back, although some more modern instruments also have two extra small fingerholes in the front. There are two main schools of shakuhachi, the *Kinko* with a trapezoid shaped buffalo horn or ivory insert in the mouthpiece, and the *Tozan* with a crescent shaped mouthpiece.

Playing the Shakuhachi
The shakuhachi is held at almost a forty-five degree angle directly in front of the body. This allows the bottom lip to rest inside the aperture, as the top lip protrudes forward slightly to channel the air down toward the sharp edge of the mouthpiece. The shakuhachi can be played fully chromatically by half or partial holing the fingerholes, and/or by raising or lowering the head, to get a semitone or even slightly higher pitch. There are a wealth of sounds available on the shakuhachi. The course airy sound is produced with a loose embouchure, while a very pure tone is produced with a tight embouchure and by moving closer to the mouthpiece. Vibrato and other techniques can be produced by shaking the head sideways at various speeds and intensities. Other techniques include running a finger rapidly over one or more holes, exploding into a tone with a lot of air, or reducing the amount of air so that only overtones can be heard.

Fingering Chart

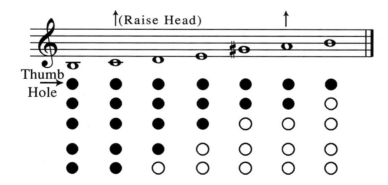

Kamakawa (CD TRACK 52)   Traditional

Suling - Indonesia

The suling is an Indonesian ring flute used in the gamelan orchestra, smaller ensembles and occasionally as a solo instrument. The suling is called a ring flute as it has a rattan ring around the top of the instrument to act as a mouthpiece to direct the air towards the fipple. It traditionally is made from bamboo in a variety of sizes from two foot long, to the larger and quite rare, yard or meter long instruments. Each region of Indonesia has a distinctive instrument with those from Bali and Java the most common. Javanese suling tend to be much thinner than those in Bali. Artists in Bali are making many ornamental versions that are carved or painted, which often are extremely beautiful visually, though not effective performance instruments. The Javanese suling style and in particular that of the Sunda region is the most musically beautiful. In Java there are both four and six holed suling, with the later providing much more versatility for the western performer.

Playing the Suling
The suling is blown from the end, being careful not to put the bottom lip past the bottom of the mouthpiece. The Balinese suling is played using circular breathing, and a distinctive technique is achieved by moving the jaw almost in a chewing action to change the timbre of the instrument. The Javanese suling is blown similar to the Balinese, but with a radically different form of ornamentation. The Javanese style focuses on expressive embellished phrases, and seldom uses circular breathing. Indonesian scales use slightly different pitches from western scales but a rough equivalent are slendro - re, fa, so, la, do; pelog degung - do, mi, fa, so, ti; and sorog - fa, la, ti, do, mi.

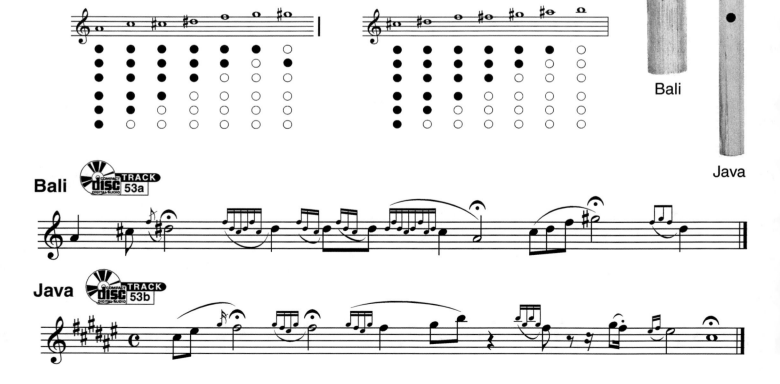

62

Tarka - Chile, Bolivia

The tarka is an Andean end-blown flute that can have a plain or ornately carved rectangular body. Tarkas come in three sizes, with the middle size tuned a fifth above the largest, and the smallest an octave above the largest. It is traditionally used for weddings and ritual ceremonies, or to bring dry weather. Many people have tarkas on their shelf, which they think are not good instruments, due to the lack of a clear tone and a good second octave. Usually most of these instruments are quite playable if the proper technique is used.

Playing the Tarka
The tarka is overblown to produce both the fundamental and the overtone simultaneously, and the sound is quite rough and coarse. Usually tarkas are played in pairs or larger groupings, and melodies in parallel fifths are common. The music is usually quite lively to accompany dancing.

Fingering Chart

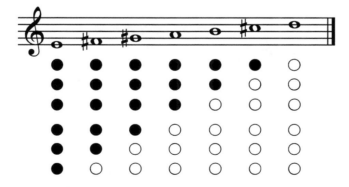

Sad Tinku　TRACK 54

Traditional

Wot - Thailand

Found in the Isaan region of Northeast Thailand and Laos, the wot is a circular panpipe arranged around a central core. All references to the wot say that it was originally a toy swung through the air, but this may be a myth since the current wot does not sound in this manner. Wot used to be played in small ensembles or as personal instruments, but have now become a very popular tourist instrument. Wot are tuned to a pentatonic scale of la, ti, do, me, fa.

Playing the Wot

Wot are not difficult to play as long as all the pipes are in good working order. The rounded center section of the wot is placed under the bottom lip and the wot is angled forward to almost a forty-five degree angle. The top lip protrudes slightly to channel the air into the pipes. The instrument is turned to get different notes and a good player creates ornamentation by moving between adjacent pipes and rapidly twirling the instrument while blowing. If the wot is out of tune, a few grains of rice dropped into the bottom of a pipe will raise its pitch, and these can be fastened by coating them with a touch of glue.

Fingering Charts

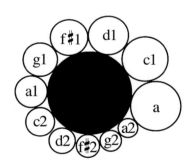

Kalasin

64

Xun - China

The xun is an ancient Chinese vessel flute made from clay that resembles an egg with a flattened bottom. Is comes in a variety of sizes, all with a large hole on the top to blow into and five or more fingerholes on the front usually spaced in parallel rows to fit the fingers, and sometimes thumb holes on the back. The xun is between four to five thousand years old, and had almost disappeared in China until it was revived in the early 20th century. The xun can be used as a solo instrument or in small ensembles.

Playing the Xun

The xun is blown into like a panpipe, by blowing down into the aperture. The fingerholes are often positioned more for aesthetics than pitch, so finding the exact finger arrangement for each instrument may take some time. Usually some compensation must take place by tilting the instrument forward or back to raise or lower the pitch. Most instruments are only capable of an octave but there are some that can get a few notes higher, and more fingerholes on the instrument do not always equate with more notes, so be careful. It can be played chromatically by partial holing and by adjusting the angle of blowing.

Fingering Chart

Rear Holes →

```
      3 5
7       6
      2 4
        1
```

```
7  ● ● ● ● ● ● ● ○
6  ● ● ● ● ● ● ○ ○
5  ● ● ● ● ● ○ ○ ○
4  ● ● ● ● ○ ○ ○ ○
3  ● ● ● ○ ○ ○ ○ ○
2  ● ● ○ ○ ○ ○ ○ ○
1  ● ○ ○ ○ ○ ○ ○ ○
   E F G A B c d e
```

Guan Shan Yue disc TRACK 56

Traditional

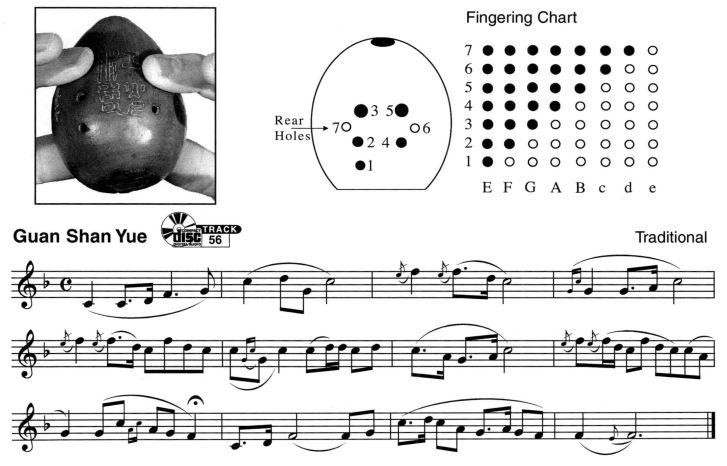

Zampona or Zamponia - Peru, Chile, Bolivia

Zamponia is the generic name for the double rowed panpipes of the Andes. Zamponia come in four sizes, ranging from over two yards or meters to just the length of a hand. Traditionally, each row of the zamponia was played by a separate musician with the melody moving back and forth between the performers, but now it is common to see one musician playing both rows as a single instrument. Zamponia are often performed in ensembles consisting of at least two or three different sizes, or in conjunction with guitars, charango, and quena. Internationally, the sound of the zamponia has become the most characteristic sound of the Andes.

Playing the Zamponia

Playing the zamponia is a bit of a challenge at first, as a player has to alternate back and forth between the rows to play the consecutive notes of a scale, and an octave of a note will be on the opposite row. It takes a bit of practice to learn where all the notes are. Usually the instrument is held so the row farther away from the performer is slightly raised so that it can be positioned quickly in front of the mouth by tilting the instrument towards the performer. Some performers will hold the pipes steady and move their head, while others hold their head steady and move the instrument. Variations of tone are produced through not sounding the pipe completely to get a variety of air sounds, as well as varying the speed and repetition of the air pulse. Partially covering a hole with the lips while playing will flatten a note.

Tuning the Zamponia

Although the pipes of the zamponia are cut to size, often they are slightly out of tune with other instruments and they can be adjusted by dropping either rice or pop-

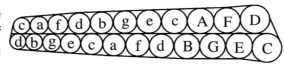

corn into the pipes to raise the pitch. Some performers will drop a touch of glue carefully into the pipe to secure the rice or popcorn while most prefer the option of altering the tuning whenever they play.

Green Firewood Traditional

Bawu - China

The bawu is a single pipe free reed of the Miao, Yi and Hani peoples of southern China. It is made from bamboo with a brass reed, and has seven main fingerholes and sometimes one extra small hole used to help tune the last note. Bawu have become a mainstream Chinese instrument, found in many ensembles and orchestras. Modern bawu often come in two keys of F and G, and better quality instrument are made in two intersecting sections so that they can be moved to adjust the pitch.

Playing the Bawu

Bawu are held like a transverse flute with the mouth fully surrounding the brass reed. They are blown with a fairly firm, fully supported supply of air, if played too softly, the reed will not sound. Bawu only uses exhalation to sound the reed, with dynamics and vibrato created both through the diaphragm and through moving a finger near an open hole. Bawu can be tongued but typically accents are created by firmly striking a fingerhole or with rapid grace notes. Bawu are constructed diatonically but usually played pentatonically, and are only capable of playing an octave plus one tone.

Fingering Chart

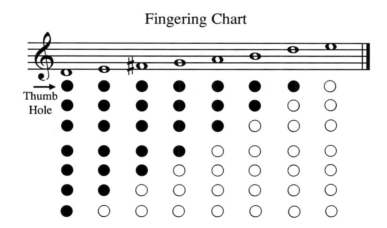

Xie Qu Yuan

Hulusi - China

The hulusi, also known as a *poleweng, baihongliao* or *bilangdao*, is a two or three pipe free reed from southern China played by the Dai, A'chang, De'ang and Wa people. It is made from a gourd wind chamber, which covers a single free reed inserted into each of the two pipes that sound. The third pipe of the hulusi does not sound. The melody pipe has six fingerholes on the front and a thumbhole on the back. The drone pipe is sometime stopped, and occasionally has one finger hole to change the drone pitch. The hulusi has gained popularity in the last twenty years both in China and internationally.

Playing the Hulusi
The hulusi is easy to play but requires a firm and steady supply of air. If not blown hard enough, it will not sound properly. The hulusi traditionally uses circular breathing, especially when using the drone. Grace notes, vibrato, glissandi and bent notes are very common and are achieved with the skillful use of the fingers.

Fingering Chart

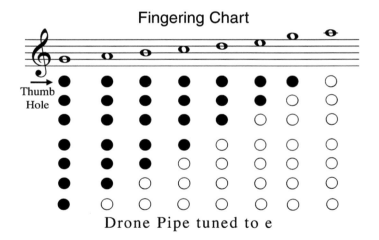

Drone Pipe tuned to e

Cui Hu

TRACK 59

Keluri - Sarawak, Malaysia

Keluri is one of many names for the bamboo free reed mouth organ played by the Orang Ulu or upriver people of Sarawak, the western state of Malaysia on the island of Borneo. Keluri are made from six pipes of different lengths held together in a tight circular bundle, one end inserted into a gourd wind chamber. Each pipe has a single free reed. The Iban instrument has a very long low-pitched pipe; the Bidayuh instrument has a larger gourd, and the Kenyan and Kayan instruments often have an additional resonator at the end of the longest pipe. Traditionally the keluri was a very important instrument used in many celebratory events, leading line dances, processions going to and from headhunting raids, as well as for entertainment. The keluri is related to the Chinese *sheng* and Thai *naw.*

Playing the Keluri
The keluri is held in the palms of both hands with the left hand closest to the body. The only difficulty in playing the keluri is that the palm side of the knuckle at the base of the left index finger plays the hole to the left of the long pipe, this can be quite awkward for those that do not have flexible joints. The tip of the left index also closes the longest pipe at the back, with the thumb closing the hole on the front pipe, and the third finger closing the hole to the right of the front pipe. The right middle finger closes the hole on the pipe to the left of the front pipe, and the thumb the hole on the pipe to the right of the front pipe. Usually the long pipe is used as a drone and kept closed. The keluri is played rhythmically with interweaving melodies and chords.

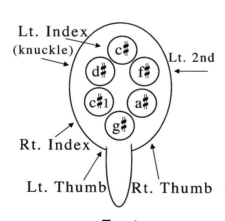

Front

Long Laput

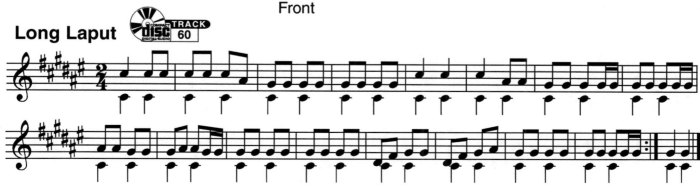

Khaen - Thailand

The khaen is a free reed bamboo mouth organ from Laos and northeast Thailand, also occasionally found in parts of northern Vietnam and southern China. Traditionally the khaen is used to accompany a form of social singing with improvisational elements called *Lam*. Each pipe contains a small brass or silver reed traditionally made by hammering a small coin on an elephant thighbone until it is paper thin and then cut to size. The most common khaen, called the khaen paat, has sixteen pipes and is anywhere from two to three and a half feet in length. The eighteen pipe version, the khaen gao, that reached six feet and more in length, is no longer played due to the simple fact that it was too long to carry on a motorcycle (so say many khaen players in Thailand!). The small six-pipe khaen hok is considered a toy, yet it can easily produce a surprising amount of music. There were older khaen with fourteen pipes that were around the same length as the khaen paat, but these are seldom seen now. There are many khaen found in tourist shops that have a lot of pipes but are only a foot or a hundred cm. long. These are not real instruments and usually cannot be played.

Playing the Khaen
The pipes of the khaen are arranged in two rows that extend through both sides of the wind chamber. The player holds the wind chamber between the palms and closes the small holes slightly above the wind chamber with the fingers to create a sound. It is played in one of five different modes determined by blocking the holes on two pipes with pitch or wax, called *kisoot*, to form drones. The complex note arrangements of the khaen allow for a good player to play a melody, countermelody, chords and rhythm simultaneously. An important part of this music is that the feel of the music can switch from a 6/8 to a 2/4 and back again, and that the emphasis is often not on the first beat of the bar, but on the last.

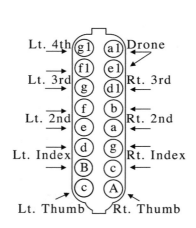

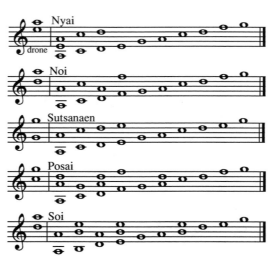

Kao Yai

Naw - Thailand

The naw, known as the *hulusheng* in southern China, is found in the mountains of northern Southeast Asia and southern China, played by minority peoples of the region including the Yi, Lahu and Lisu. The naw is the oldest member of the Asian mouth organ family, dating back at least four thousand years. It has five pipes grouped in a circular cluster, whose open ends appear flush with the bottom of the gourd wind chamber, allowing the player to "bend" the notes by slowly covering the ends of the pipes with the right thumb while playing. Traditionally this instrument was used to accompany dance, to lead festive events and to play a coded language for unmarried people to converse with.

Playing the Naw

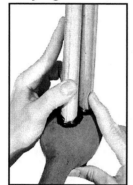

The naw is held in the left hand between the base of the left thumb on the front and the last two fingers at the back. The left index finger closes the fingerhole on the longest pipe to the left. The left thumb closes the hole on the front pipe. The left middle finger closes the both pipes at the back with the fingertip and second finger pad respectively. The fingerhole on the pipe to the right is closed by the right index finger. The right thumb is the secret to the naw, as it either closes or partially closes the ends of the pipes on the underside of the gourd, thereby dropping the pitch to obtain other notes. This is very important, as the second note of the scale can only obtained by closing both the fingerhole and the end of the front pipe. Both vibrato and bent notes are obtained by the use of the right thumb under the pipes.

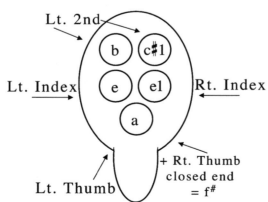

Lt. 2nd

b   c#1

Lt. Index   e   e1   Rt. Index

a

Lt. Thumb

+ Rt. Thumb
closed end
= f#

Kuu Kup

(drone)

Sheng - China

The sheng is a free reed bamboo mouth organ traditionally used in both court and folk music in China. In the last fifty years it has become a standard instrument in modern Chinese orchestras. The traditional sheng has from fourteen to seventeen pipes with a diatonic scale. More modern instruments have up to thirty-six pipes and are tuned chromatically. The sheng's pipes are in a circular configuration, but there are also sheng with the pipes arranged in three parallel rows called *fangsheng*. The sheng has a long history in China, dating back almost three thousand years with instruments in the eighth century bearing a surprising resemblance to modern instruments. The sheng is the precursor to the accordion, harmonica, concertina, and reed organ.

Playing the Sheng
The sheng is held between the heels of both hands so that the fingers are free to move between pipes. The right index finger reaches inside to play two fingerholes on the inner side of the pipes. The reeds sound the same pitch on inhalation and exhalation, and accents are created with both the diaphragm and tongue. Traditionally, the sheng plays melodies and chords simultaneously, punctuated by multiple tonguing techniques, large or rapid crescendos and flutterings of the diaphragm.

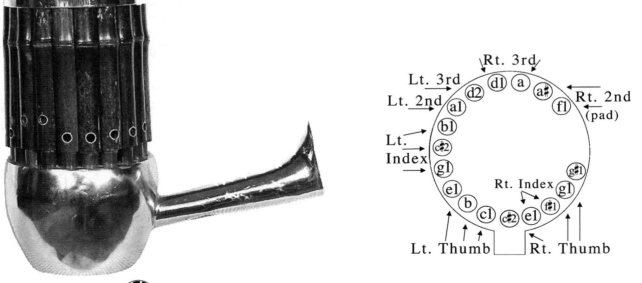

Feng Huang TRACK 63

Sumpoton - Sabah, Malaysia

The sumpoton is a bamboo free reed mouth organ from Sabah, the eastern state of Malaysia on the island of Borneo. The Kadazan and Dusun peoples use the sumpoton as a personal instrument, for celebrations, and for ceremonies. It is made of eight bamboo pipes in two parallel rows that are inserted at one end into a gourd wind chamber. Sumpoton are often played together in large ensembles, or played with other bamboo instruments as part of the bamboo ensembles. The sumpoton ranges in size from the length of a hand to the length of an arm.

Playing the Sumpoton
The sumpoton is held between the heel and last three fingers of the left hand so that the thumb can close both fingerholes on the front of the instrument and the index finger can close the one fingerhole on the back of the instrument. The first three fingers of the right hand close the tops of the last three pipes on the right, and the last pipe can rest on the right little finger for added support. The third pipe on the left is a drone pipe and usually does not have a finger hole. There are three playing positions for the sumpoton: vertical, horizontal under the left arm, and inverted. The inverted position is quite popular especially when playing a longer instrument, as the drone pipe can be stopped against the upper thigh.

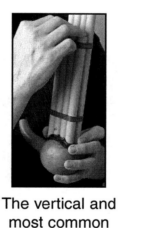

The vertical and most common position

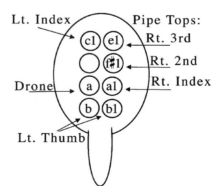

The horizontal position

The inverted position

Maliau TRACK 64

(drone)

(2nd time with variation)

73

Didjeridu - Australia

The didjeridu is the wooden horn of the aboriginal people of Australia. The didjeridu has become an extremely popular instrument worldwide. Originally it was
a sacred instrument played only by men whom had gone through a rigorous ini-
tiation rite and had spent years in learning the songs and stories of their people. There are still many people who believe that the didjeridu should not be
taken lightly and should only be played by the initiated. Traditionally, the didjeridu is made from a type of eucalyptus tree that has been naturally hollowed
out by termites. Presently there are commercial didjeridu made from bamboo,
cactus and plastic. Good quality instruments have a narrow bore and flare to a
natural bell.

Playing the Didjeridu
The didjeridu is blown from the narrow end, with very loose lips that vibrate to the
fundamental pitch of the instrument. The fundamental must be sounded very clearly without any extra air sound, or the full potential of the didjeridu cannot be reached.
Many beginners tighten their lips too much as if they were going to play a trumpet,
actually the didjeridu requires a very loose yet still controlled embouchure. The
tongue is used to create accents by making "d" or "t" or "k" sounds or to block the
hole really quickly and then release it to make a spit sound or a hoot. Hoots are
made with a tight embouchure like blowing a trumpet. Advanced players can play
two or more pitched hoots. There are two different ranges of sounds produced on
the didjeridu, depending if the player's cheeks are held puffed out or are held in
tightly. With tightened cheeks the tongue is pulled back and forth slowly to sound
harmonics. The player's voice is also used to add many animal yells, the most common of which are the *kookaburra* and *dingo*. The didjeridu uses circular breathing,
and is a good instrument to learn it on.

Jabba

Dung Chen - Tibet

The dung chen is a long collapsible metal Tibetan horn usually played in pairs. Dung chen are an integral part of many forms of Tibetan ritual music and are often played with smaller horns, drums and double reeds. Because of their length, some instrument reaching over nine feet or three meters, they create a low powerful sound. Dung chen have become popular outside of Tibet, due to the exportation of lighter copper instruments from Nepal. Older dung chen are made from brass and silver, and much heavier.

Playing the Dung Chen
Dung chen can be played sitting or standing, and the bell is placed either on the floor, a small stand, or on the shoulder of a seated monk. The dung chen is blown like a trumpet but with a much more dynamic embouchure. There are no valves or any other way to change notes, so all the pitches on the dung chen are produced with the lips. Dung chen do not play many of the higher pitches in the overtone series, mainly the tonic, the fifth, and the first octave. Typical long phrases start low, rising in pitch, playing a deep vibrato, and then finish either with a quick lower or higher tone. These are often interspersed with short rising pitches.

Linkha TRACK 66

75

Pu, Dung, or Conch - Polynesia, Tibet, India

Conch shells are used in many cultures around the world as a signal or cere-monial horn and known by a variety of names. Conch horns are believed to be very old instruments and are traced back to the Stone Age. Pu is the Polynesian term for conch trumpets used as signal horns. Dung is the Tibetan term for conch horns usually covered in silver and semi precious stones and used for religious ceremonies.

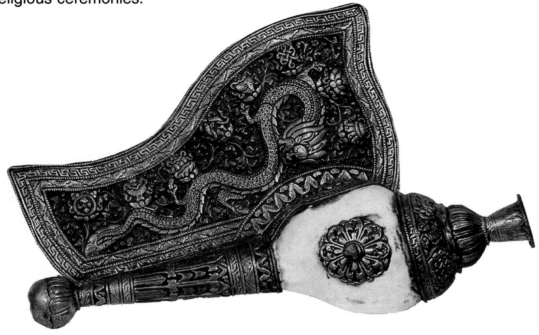

Playing the Pu

The pu is either blown from the side or from the end, depending where the blow hole is located. Tibetan dung have a mouthpiece built in the end, but other conches have the end of the shell cut off. The instrument is blown like a trum-pet, so changes in the tightness of the embouchure can create higher pitched notes. Other pitches are created by placing the fingers inside the opening of the shell if it is large, or over top of the opening if it is small. Some instruments are capable of five or six pitches. Some smaller conch, like those found in India, are played more at the side of the mouth where the lips are thinner.

Malaa 🔘 TRACK 67

Duduk - Armenia

The duduk is an Armenian tubular double reed that is also known as *mey* in Turkey, played by Kurds and Turkmen, and as *balaban* in Iraq and Iran. Tubular double reeds have a much softer mellow sound, as compared to conical double reeds, and are used to accompany singing or in instrumental laments. The duduk has become quite popular in the West especially in film music, and instruments are readily available for purchase online. Care must be taken to get a good quality instrument, and an especially good quality reed. The pitch of a duduk can change if a different reed is used, so it is important to get a replacement reed from the same maker. Duduki only have slightly more than a single octave range and are made diatonically but are capable of playing chromatically by half holing.

Playing the Duduk

The duduk is played by putting just the tip of the reed into the mouth, and blowing with a smooth pressure from the diaphragm. Vibrato is achieved from a subtle movement of the bottom lip or from the diaphragm. Although most duduki have eight holes in the front, many players only use seven of these them, leaving the bottom one open. Duduki reeds must be tuned so the note sounded with six fingers on, is an octave lower than the note with all fingers off. Fine-tuning is achieved by either increasing or decreasing the number of threads on the reed so it can be placed shallower or deeper into the instrument, or by adjusting the collar on the reed. To play an ascending scale, the notes of the duduk are uncovered from the bottom of the instrument to the top in succession, except that the rear thumb-hole is uncovered before the top hole on the front.

Fingering Chart

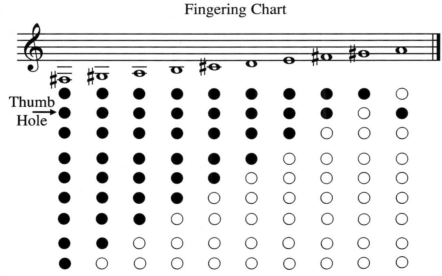

Lament TRACK 68

Traditional

Guanzi and Bili - China

The Chinese bili and guanzi are two related conical double reeds that have descended from the Armenian duduk family. Bili are made from bamboo with a soft reed and guanzi are made from rosewood with a hard reed. Often the terms bili and guanzi are used interchangeably. The bili was widely used in Chinese court music and is closer to the original instrument that came from the West, while the guanzi is considered a folk instrument and is now primarily used in Buddhist and other folk music genres.

Playing the Guanzi and Bili
Adjusting the reed properly for both instruments is important. The pitches of the guanzi are usually quite well set, although the reed usually requires sanding to adjust. The edge of bili reeds must be sanded, hardened by putting a hot knife against the wet reed for a short time, and then a shallow line cut into the side of the reed without going all the way through the side. Both instruments require circular breathing and a solid support from the diaphragm. Notes can be bent by arching the fingers off the fingerholes or by changing the length of reed in the mouth. The bili tends to have a much broader vibrato than the guanzi. The second octave on both instruments is a challenge and requires more air pressure, more lip pressure on the reed, positioning the reed farther in the mouth, and sometimes half-holing the back hole on the guanzi.

Fingering Chart

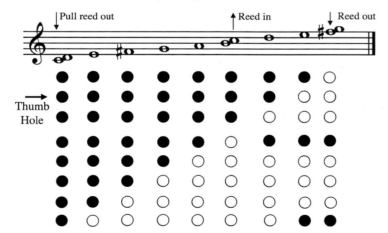

Bili

Guanzi

Mu Dan

Midjweh and Arghul - Egypt

The midjweh or *midjwiz,* and arghul are double pipe, single reed, folk clarinets that are found in many parts of the Middle East by a number of other names. They are made from two hollow reed pipes strung together side by side. Two smaller reeds are cut at the nodes and inserted into the ends of the pipes, and a single cut is made into these to create the vibrating reeds. The ancestor of the clarinet, midjweh have a history of more than four thousand years in Egypt. Midjweh have changed little over time, and it is interesting to note that midjweh reeds are identical to those still used in the Indian snake charmer and the drone pipes of the Scottish bagpipe.

Playing the Midjweh and Arghul
To play, the vibrating reeds are placed completely in the mouth and both pipes are sounded at once with a very strong pressure from the diaphragm. The arghul has fingerholes on only pipe and the other is a drone, so the breath pressure must remain constant to maintain a steady drone. The midjweh has fingerholes in parallel on both pipes and the pipes are played in unison by placing the fingers so that the finger can cover the two adjacent holes on each pipe. Circular breathing is employed, although quite awkward, as the reeds inside the mouth do not easily allow any room for the tongue to move. Usually a performer must first work hard to overcome a gag reflex just by having the reeds in the mouth and a much greater gag reflex trying to circular breathe.

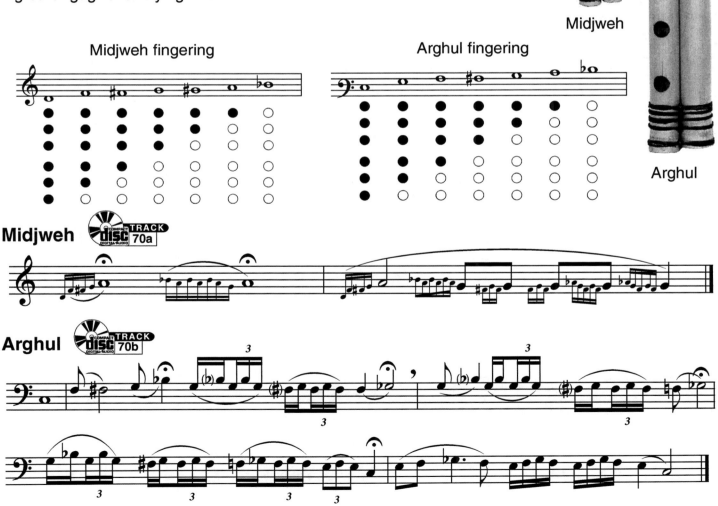

Midjweh

Arghul

Midjweh fingering

Arghul fingering

Midjweh TRACK 70a

Arghul TRACK 70b

79

Pungi or Bin - India

The pungi, more commonly known as the snake charmer, is a double-piped folk clarinet with single reeds. It has either a gourd or wooden wind chamber that surrounds the reeds and is fixed in place with beeswax. The pungi has identical reeds to those of the Egyptian *midjweh* and is likely a descendant, with the wind chamber being added to assist with circular breathing. Usually the pungi is played to mesmerize cobra snakes, but as snakes do not have ears, it is more likely the shape of the wind chamber, which is made to resemble the flared head of a cobra, that makes the snake respond to the instrument. The pungi has one melody pipe, and one drone, which on some pungi is adjustable. Some modern pungi have two drones.

Playing the Pungi

Pungi are not difficult to play as long as the reeds are adjusted properly, which often entails taking the gourd off to place a small hair under each reed to lift them up a bit to sound. Circular breathing is essential to playing the pungi, which means that the reeds must be adjusted well and the gourd must be completely sealed. If the reeds are too tight to circular breathe and adjusting with a hair does not work, then the reeds may need to be shaved to make thinner and lighter. This should be done with extreme caution as it is important not to create a large gap between the reed and the body, or the reed will not sound. The instrument is usually played with a steady drone and short repetitive melodies. The pungi must be blown with a very firm and steady stream of air, as too little air pressure will not sound the reeds properly.

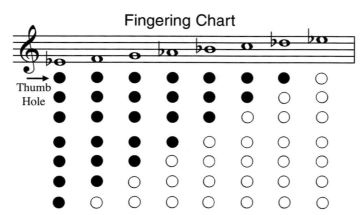

Fingering Chart

Selaiyu TRACK 71

(drone)

Suona or Sona - China

The suona is the Chinese conical double reed that was traditionally used for outdoor music activities or military purposes, and has now become a concert instrument. The suona descended from the Middle Eastern *shenai* or *zurna*, and was brought to China along the Silk Road, probably first as a military instrument. Suona have a brass bell connecting to a scalloped wooden body, on top of which is a metal mouthpiece that holds a small double reed of cane. Suona range in size from small to large and are very loud.

Playing the Suona
Proper preparation of the reed is the key to playing the suona well. Although reeds are easy to find in Chinese music stores or online, they must be sanded smoothly before being used. It is also a good idea to harden the reed by first dampening it, then pressing the edge with a hot knife or an iron for a very brief period of time. It takes practice to do this well, but the reeds are very cheap and often come in large packages. Suona use circular breathing, and are often played extremely fast with great virtuosity. Built diatonically, the suona is capable of playing two or more octaves, depending on the size. Besides using common reed techniques suona often imitate bird sounds and human voices. Playing a suona in tune takes quite a bit of practice and a good ear. Most suona are made with the fingerholes evenly spaced, therefore, obtaining the correct pitch requires constant adjustments of wind pressure and the depth of the reed in the mouth.

Fingering Chart

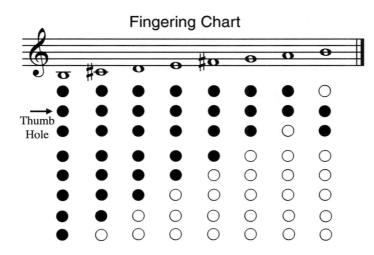

Zheng Yue Li Lai

Traditional

81

Ahoco - Ivory Coast

The ahoco is a scraper played by women in Ivory Coast to accompany songs and dances. It is made from a rounded dried fruit shell, a flattened nutshell, and a single straight wooden stick that has a spiral groove traveling three quarters the length of the body. Sometimes a string will attach all the parts, but traditionally they were not attached. Many ahoco would be played together in an ensemble while dancing. Ahoco are a very effective percussion instrument, and are increasingly popular in the West.

Playing the Ahoco
The stick is gripped by the last three fingers of the left hand. The left thumb and first finger are free to hold the flat shell by its edges so that the open end is facing the length of the stick, and the flat side can be touched to the stick. The round shell is held in the right hand and placed over the stick so that it slides along its length. The round shell is rhythmically rubbed against the stick while the flat shell alternately touches the stick to create a variety of accents. Advanced players can partially cover the hole on the flat shell with their left thumb to add different tones.

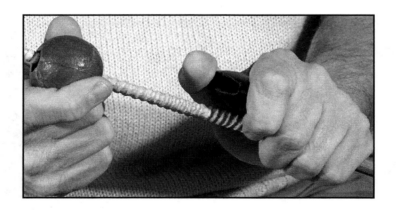

Comoe

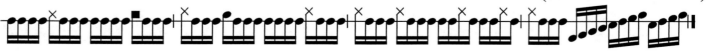

(continue with variations)

82

Aslatua, Kashaka, or Televi - Ghana

Aslatua, kashaka, or televi are three of the numerous names for a double rattle found in Ghana and surrounding countries. Aslatua are made from two small swawa gourds, with pebbles or seeds inside. The two gourds are attached to each other with a thick string. Depending on the region, aslatua are used by men, women, or children. Aslatua are capable of very complex rhythms especially when played with a set in each hand.

Playing the Aslatua, Kashaka, and Televi

One gourd of the aslatua is held high in the palm of the hand so that the string passes between the thumb and fingers close to the base of the fingers. The string is wrapped behind the fingers, as the hand is held in a slightly cupped position. The second gourd is gripped in the palm, held in place by the last two fingers. With a straight wrist, the aslatua is shaken by moving only the forearm forward and back with enough momentum so that when the little finger releases the gourd it will swing around the hand to the front side of the thumb and hit the other gourd, and then back around the hand again to hit it again from the other side. The moving gourd can be caught by the little finger at any time. This technique takes practice, and should be performed with one set of aslatua in each hand. Once a basic rhythm is established, variations can be created by whipping the gourds so that they travel around the hand faster, twirling the moving gourd so that it does not always hit the held gourd, and alternating the two hands.

Gbele TRACK 74

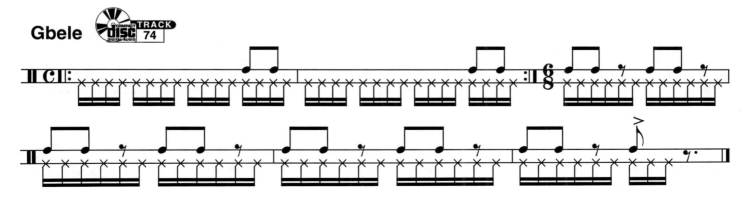

83

Balofon - West Africa

The balofon is a gourd resonated xylophone found throughout West Africa. Each gourd resonator has a small hole covered with the fibre from a spider egg sac that acts as a buzzer. The instrument is played sitting on the floor or suspended from a strap around the performer's shoulders. The balofon tradition is passed from master to student and the training in some regions is so rigorous that students can collapse from physical exhaustion.

Playing the Balofon
The balofon is struck with two mallets wrapped with rubber strapping, and often a performer wears bells on his hand as additional percussion. The techniques and rhythms are often very complex and vary from village to village and region to region. It is very important that each bar has a good buzz when struck and performers often adjust the position of the gourds to ensure a good tone. Compound rhythms are quite common.

Tuning the Balofon
Usually, balofon are tuned by an instrument maker. However, sometimes players want to adjust the balfon to new scales, and this should be done with extreme caution. The gourd resonators were chosen for the specific pitch of each bar, and altering a bar may make the resonator ineffective. Raising the pitch of a bar can be achieved by shaving the wood, preferably from the underside ends of the bar. Some adventurous folks will even shave wood from the underside centre of a bar, but this is not recommended unless practiced on other pieces of wood first. Lowering the pitch is simply achieved by adding lumps of wax to the underside ends of the bars.

Bakari

Traditional

(continue with variations)

Bendir, Dap, Def - Eurasia

Bendir, Dap, and Def are single-head hand-struck frame drums that are very common throughout parts of Europe, the Middle East and Central Asia. Frame drums are basically a narrow rim over which a skin is stretched on one side, some containing jingles either on the outside or inside of the rim. There are historic indications that frame drums may be over eight thousand years old, and they have been used in many contexts, from ritual music to entertainment. The bendir is the Moroccan frame drum with a single string across the head that acts like a snare, the dap is a Uyghur frame drum with short jingles on the inner rim, and the def is the Persian frame drum with long strands of jingles attached to the inner rim.

Playing the Bendir

Frame drums can be held on the lap but more commonly are held balanced on the palm of the left hand, held in place with the thumb at the back and the fingers being able to easily reach the skin on the front. The right hand is either free, one or two hand's width away from the left hand, or at the side of the drum with the thumb touching the drum only and being used as a pivot to either play the centre of the drum or the rim with the fingers. The position and strength of a strike on the rim can produce a variety of tones and volumes. Rolls are accomplished with either alternating single fingers on the two hands or by consecutively striking with the fingers of one hand starting with the little finger. This technique can then be alternated between hands to produce a long continuous roll. A variety of other techniques are used much like those of the dumbek.

Ziz

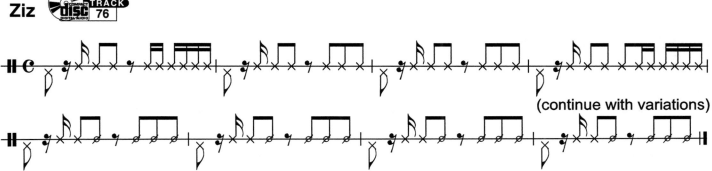

(continue with variations)

Bodhran - Ireland

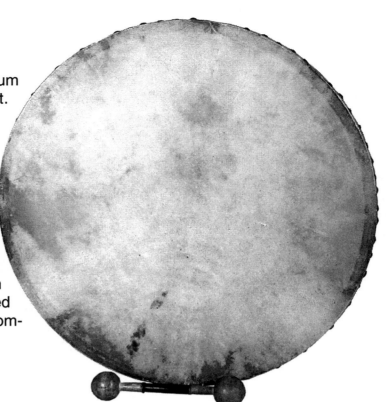

The bodhran is a single headed frame drum struck with a double-headed mallet. Bodhran were originally played in folk rituals and processional music. They have since become an important accompaniment to Celtic dance and vocal music. Bodhran have a thin circular wooden frame that is covered on one side with goatskin. Modern instruments are made with an adjustable frame so that they can be tuned. The mallet is made with two heads and a slim body, with many modern mallets having weighted heads. Bodhran are capable of very complex rhythms and techniques.

Playing the Bodhran

Bodhran are rested on the left thigh, and advanced musicians tuck part of the bodhran under the left arm to leave the left hand free. The left hand is placed on the inside of the bodhran to either partially mute the skin or to change the tone by applying slight pressure with the side of the hand on the skin, while moving up and down to get a variety of tones. The right hand holds the mallet similar to a pencil, but with a really loose wrist that is dropped forward while the forearm is held vertically. The forearm moves forward

and back flinging the wrist. If the wrist is held at the correct position in relationship to the drumhead, both the top and bottom of the mallet can strike the skin to achieve rolls and triplets. Sometimes the wooden frame is struck with the mallet to create additional accents.

Blackwood

(continue with variations)

86

Bones - Quebec, Canada

Bones are percussive clappers that are common in Celtic music and forms of American minstrel music. Although clappers have been used throughout history in many cultures, it is likely that the origins of this instrument are to be found in the Celtic tradition. In American history, bones were often used by slaves to replace banned traditional instruments. Modern bones can be found made from plastic and wood, while earlier instruments were made from animal ribs. Traditional French Canadian bones are made from cow rib.

Playing the Bones

Each bone has a slight curve and they are held with a pair in each hand with the curves facing away from each other. One bone is placed between the index and the middle finger with the concave side arching towards the thumb, and secured against the heel of the hand at the base of the thumb with the index finger. The second bone is held loosely between the second and third fingers so that the concave side faces the small finger.

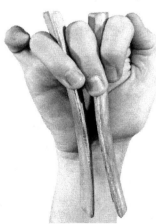

With the wrist held up at a ninety-degree angle to the arm, rotate the forearm back and forth, making a motion that resembles a child waving. The second bone should move in both directions and hit the stationary bone, and the fingers are constantly making subtle adjustments to control the bounce of the bone. With practice, very fast triplets can be obtained with each hand, as well as other intricate percussive passages between the two hands.

Franchir CD TRACK 78

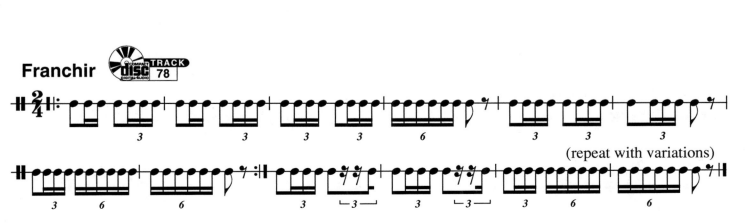

(repeat with variations)

87

Cabasa - Brazil

The cabasa is a bead scraper used in Latin American music that probably had its origins with the African shekere. Cabasa are made from tight strands of metal beads that surround a short rounded tube covered with corrugated metal attached to a handle. Cabasa are used in most Latin percussive ensembles and are also now considered a common orchestral instrument. Good players of this instrument can really add a high degree of showmanship to a performance.

Playing the Cabasa

The cabasa are held by the handle in the right hand, resting the beaded cylinder in the palm of the left hand with the left fingers lightly wrapping around the beads. Rotating the right wrist back and forth creates the rhythm. The most dynamic aspect of the cabasa is to whip it into the air to create a roll. This is achieved by flicking the right wrist very fast away from the body and at the same time quickly elevating the cabasa over the head to spin the beads, and then dropping the instrument while rotating the wrist towards the body, and finishing with the cabasa in the left palm again. With practice, the roll can be extended for quite some time. Smaller rolls and accents can be achieved by varying the degree of this movement.

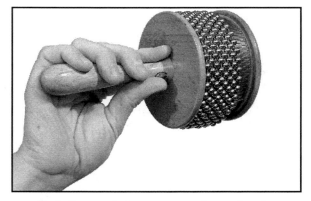

flick the wrist up, away from body

Rotate down towards body

Torção

88

Cajon - Peru, Cuba

The cajon is a box drum developed from a simple packing box played by African slaves in Peru and Cuba in place of their traditional drums. Recently, the cajon has been adopted as a standard percussion instrument in Flamenco music. Cajon now come in a variety of sizes and are made from a wide range of materials. The front of the cajon is usually loose at the top so that when struck it makes a distinctive rattling sound.

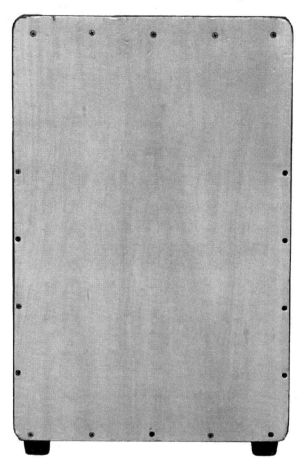

Playing the Cajon
The performer sits astride the cajon and strikes the front top edge with the fingers to produce the rattle and in the center with either the flat or heel of the hand to produce a bass tone. Some players also strike the sides with their heels to add a counter rhythm.

Flamenco Tango   Traditional

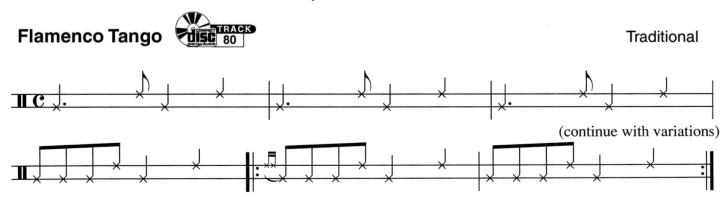

(continue with variations)

89

Changgo - Korea

The changgo is the double-headed hour-glass drum of Korea, believed to have been brought to Korea from the West along the Silk Road. The changgo is quite large and has two heads that extend well beyond the rim, the left head is made from cowhide and the right head has a thinner skin made from dog. Both heads are bound together with lacing that crosses between them, which can be adjusted for tuning. Changgo are a main drum of Korea used in many styles, from court to shamanistic folk music.

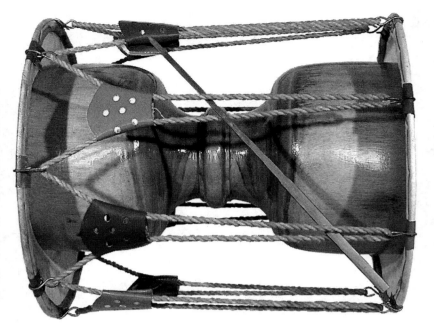

Playing the Changgo

The changgo is played in two ways, the first - seated on the floor with the drum in front of the player, common in most styles; and the second - held by a strap under the left arm for Samul Nori music where the performer also dances. In the seated position, the left hand is placed at the two o'clock position of the rim, so the rim is nestled between the thumb and fingers, and the fingers hang loosely onto the head. The right hand holds a long thin bamboo stick close to the base of the thumb so that it can bounce. Both the end and flat of this stick alternately hit the center and edge of the right head, either bouncing on the skin, or giving a very loud thwack. The left hand hits the centre of the head bouncing the fingers off to give an open sound, or leave the fingers on to give a closed sound. This style of playing is often very slow and majestic. When playing Samul Nori, the left hand holds a mallet that runs over the thumb and little finger but under the other fingers and can hit either head. The right hand uses the same bamboo stick as described above. Samul Nori style is very fast and powerful.

Seated playing position

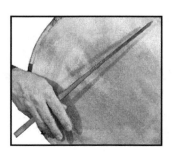

Right Hand

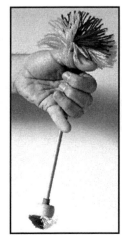

Left Hand

Insa

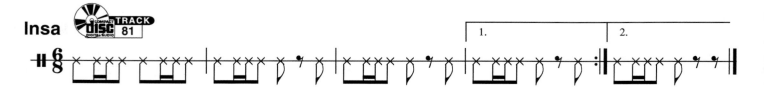

Djembe - West Africa

The djembe has become the most recognizable drum from West Africa, with a history that can be traced to the twelfth century Mali Empire and the Mandinka people. It was used as both a solo instrument or to accompany dancing and singing, at weddings, festivals or rituals. The djembe is prized for its volume, and its combination of a deep bass tone contrasted with very sharp accents. In a traditional ensemble, the djembe is usually accompanied by a pair of drums, called *dundun*, which the djembe speaks over top of. In some regions, the djembe performs a call and response with a dancer, where the djembe calls the steps to the dancer, in a complex rhythmic language not often heard in the west.

Playing the Djembe
There are three basic tones on the djembe: the bass tone, the full tone and the slap. It is important to make these three tones distinct before attempting any complex rhythms. Bouncing an almost flat closed hand just off the center of the drum produces a rich bass tone. Bouncing the closed flat fingers just inside the rim of the drum produces the full tone, and this must be adjusted to find the most resonant sound for both hands, which varies with each drum. The slap is the highest-pitched djembe sound and the technique differs per performer. With relaxed wrist and fingers, whip the hand down at a slight forty-five degree angle to the centerline so that the fingers land just inside the rim and bounce off quickly. Some players make almost a cupping motion. The result is a loud crack, and it may take some practice to get it. These three techniques are played in different combinations to produce all the traditional rhythms.

Playing the full tone

Bass tone

The slap

Bpene    Traditional

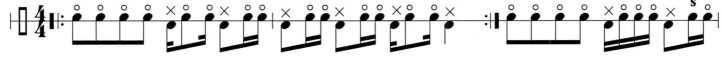

o = open; x = closed; s = slap or accented

Dumbek or Darabuka - Middle East

The dumbek is a Middle Eastern goblet drum found in many forms and known by many names. Made from wood, clay or metal, it has a large head and a slim waist that flares to an opening at the bottom. Dumbek have single heads made from goat, fish and occasionally snake skin, with many modern instruments having plastic heads. Dumbek are used in a wide range of ensembles in both classical and folk music. The dumbek has become a very popular drum worldwide.

Playing the Dumbek
There are many regional variations of playing styles, which are all worth exploring. Commonly the dumbek is held gripped under the left arm, or resting on the left thigh. The left hand rests on top so the fingers can comfortably hang over the top rim. The right hand is free to play the right rim very close to the edge to get the "bek" sound, or to play the centre of the drum to get the low resonant "dum" sound. There are a variety of techniques that include: snapping the fingers consecutively onto the drum; rolls done on the finger tips; rolling the finger nails on the centre of the head; a roll alternating the thumb and little finger; and drop rolls where the fingers are dropped on to the drum in succession starting from the little finger, which done on both hands creates a very fast light roll.

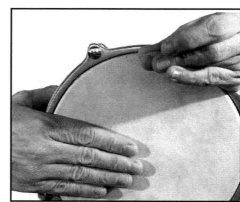

Right hand playing a "dum"

Left hand preparing to snap a "bek"

Baladi

Traditional
(continue with variations)

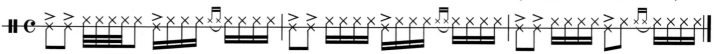

92

Ektara or Gopiyantra - India, Bangladesh

The ektara is a one-string tension drum that is played by the Baul people of Bengal and Bangladesh, to accompany religious songs. It is made from a gourd or small round wooden container that is open at both ends. The bottom is covered with an animal skin, which is pierced at the center, through which runs a gut or metal string. The string runs through the center of the container and continues up to attach to a peg head between two long slats of thin wood, which are attached to the side of the container. The term ektara translates directly as *one string.*

Playing the Ektara
The ektara can be held under an arm or placed on the lap, so that the left fingers and thumb can push the two slats together, while the right hand plucks the string with any type of plectrum. Pushing the slats together releases the tension of the string, thereby lowering the pitch. Various sounds are produced by varying the tension while plucking the ektara, including: a number of individual pitches, large and small glissandi, and a very powerful deep percussive sound produced when the string is totally slack.

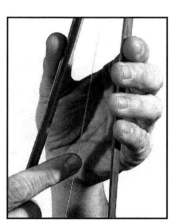

Left hand squeezing the sides together as the right hand plucks

Kuakata CD TRACK 84

(continue with variations)

93

Kayamba - Kenya

The kayamba is a mat or raft rattle used to accompany songs and dances in Kenya. It is made from two bunches of reeds bound together to make two rafts that are themselves bound together with seeds or small beads put in between. The kayamba has become a popular rattle in the West and is available in many sizes. Recently kayamba have been made with handles, as very few people in the west know the proper playing technique.

Playing the Kayamba
Holding the arms and wrists straight while pointing towards the floor, hold the kayamba lengthways between the two hands so that the ends of the instrument are cradled in slightly bent fingers. The thumbs lie on top of the instrument to strike the kayamba as it is flung quickly back and forth into the fingers of the other hand. This is such a fast and loose process that the kayamba almost floats as it moves back and forth. The thumbs beat out a variety of accents as the rattle moves rapidly between the hands.

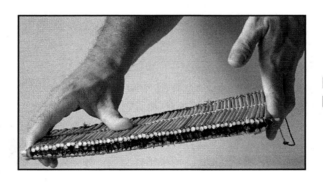

Holding the
Kayamba

Samburu TRACK 85

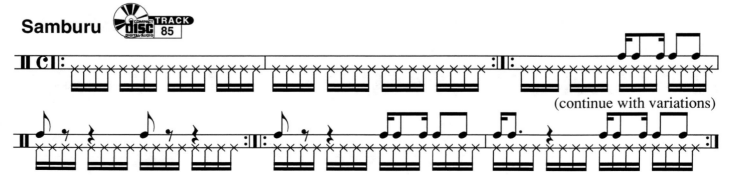

(continue with variations)

Komok or Anadalahari - India, Bangladesh

The komok or anadalahari is a plucked tension drum of the Baul people of Bengal and Bangladesh. It has a small wooden drum-like body with a loose hide top, at the centre of which is attached a string that runs through the inside of the drum to reach approximately a hand length beyond the mouth of the drum. A bell shaped metal handle is attached at the end of the string. Komok are used by itinerant musicians singing devotional songs, usually as part of an ensemble. There are also two string versions of the komok played as if they had only one string.

Playing the Komok

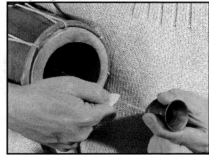

The komok is held with the elbow under the arm, while the handle is held between the thumb and fingers of either the same or opposite hand. The string is plucked with a plectrum held in the hand that is not holding the handle. A good player can create complex rhythms, with rapid and occasionally explosive gestures that have a surprisingly vocal quality.

Sundari

(continue with variations)

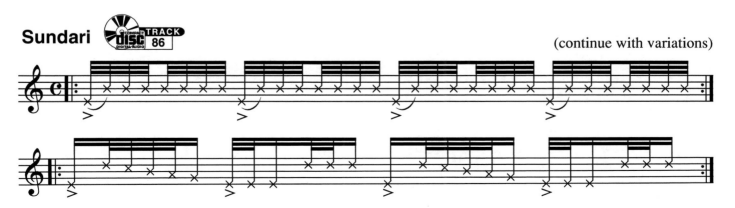

95

Oyo - Nigeria

Oyo are basket rattles from Nigeria with a conical rattle woven around either a gourd or metal base, and a handle at the top. Seeds, small stones and occasionally pieces of metal are placed inside. Oyo are typically made as a double basket rattle although there are single basket versions. Oyo have a very distinctive sound that carries well even in large ensembles.

Playing the Oyo

The oyo is held horizontally between the thumb and fingers so that the handles face the back of the hand. There are three positions to play the oyo: the neutral position with the flat bottom of the oyo facing the player, the forward position where the base faces forward and the back position where the base faces back. The oyo is shaken from the forearm with a rigid wrist, and is then turned to the forward and back positions to create varying accents. Often two oyo are played together, one in each hand.

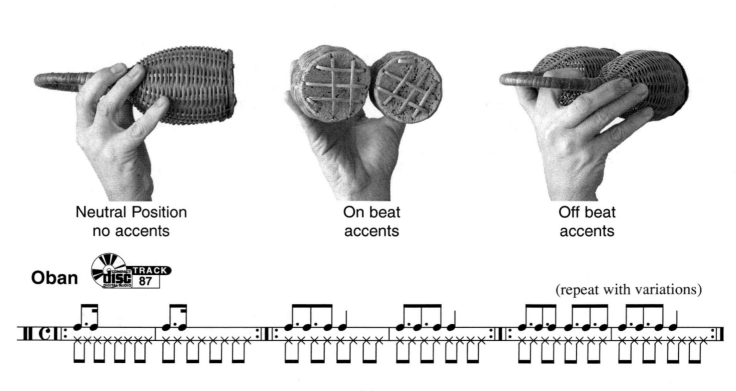

Neutral Position
no accents

On beat
accents

Off beat
accents

Oban TRACK 87

(repeat with variations)

Pandeiro - Brazil

The pandeiro is a single headed tambourine that came to Brazil with the Portuguese. Traditionally, the Brazilian pandeiro had an animal hide head and did not have jingles, but modern instruments have plastic tops and jingles. The pandeiro has a very distinctive playing style that makes it a highly versatile percussion instrument used in a wide variety of Brazilian music.

Playing the Pandeiro
There are three basic strokes for playing the pandero: fingertips, thumb and base of hand. They are played on the skin by the right hand while the instrument is held almost horizontally with the left hand. A basic combination starts with the fingertips held together and striking the skin firmly, quickly followed by a strike with the side of the thumb, then a strike with the heel of the hand and finally with another thumb strike. This is performed in a smooth succession, with a slight rocking

motion of the hand and should become very rapid. There are many different combinations and variations of these strokes depending on the rhythm and accents desired. There are also many other techniques including slapping the skin with the flat of the hand or pressing your thumb into the skin as you run it around the rim to get a roll.

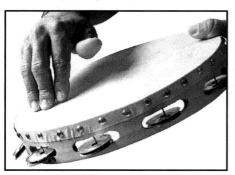
Fingertips

Thumb

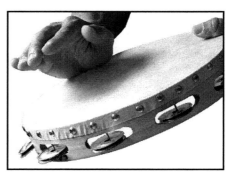
Base of hand

Salsa

o = open; x = closed with jingle sound; s = slap on skin

Senh Tien or Sinh Tien - Vietnam

The senh tien is a combined clapper, rasp, and jingle made from three pieces of wood and old Chinese coins. It was used in the Vietnamese Nguyen Court from the early nineteenth century and has since found its way into a number of other musical styles. The main body of the senh tien is made from two wooden slats that are partially glued together with the bottom hinged by a piece of leather. The bottom slat has corrugated grooves cut into the underside, with coins attached to the upper side by a long bolt. The top slat has two bolts, each with coins attached to the end, so that the bolts of the top and bottom slats line-up when held together. The wooden striker is held in the opposite hand and has corrugated grooves cut into one side. The senh tien is quite an effective percussive instrument that easily fits with many styles of music.

Playing the Senh Tien
The senh tien is held in the left hand with the thumb resting on the top slat and the index finger on the corrugated part of the bottom slat. The remaining fingers hold the main body. The index finger controls the hinged section of the bottom slat, which is used to strike the top slat. The striker is held in the right hand and can either hit the main body, scrape the grooves on the bottom slat, or stroke its corrugated edge along the side of the upper slat. Combinations of all these techniques can be used in simple and complex rhythmic patterns.

Song Da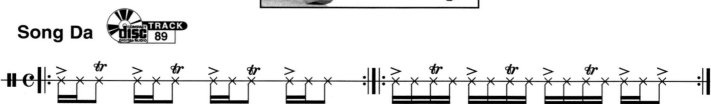

98

Shekere - Uganda

The shekere is one of the many names for gourd net rattles found in Africa and Latin America. Originating mainly as a woman's instrument, they are now played by anyone in many forms of music. Shekere are made from a gourd surrounded by a net interwoven with shell or glass beads throughout. Usually the webbing is quite loose with a tail-like end piece without beads. Some instruments have tighter webbing without a tail.

Playing the Shekere

There are two ways to play the shekere, that vary with a loose or tight weave. On instruments with a loose weave, the right hand grips the handle of the gourd, and the left hand holds the tail of the webbing at the other end of the instrument. The left hand varies tension on the webbing by pulling and slackening the webbing while the right hand moves the gourd laterally back and forth to create the rhythm. Sometimes the right hand makes a circular motion or the left hand rapidly pulls the webbing to give rhythmic variation and accents. Instruments with a tight weave are cradled between the two hands with the fingers tapping on the beads to create rhythmic patterns. Advanced players often juggle the instrument between the hands and strike the bottom of the gourd to create more rhythmic complexity.

Left hand gripping the tail as the
right hand moves the handle

Kidepo

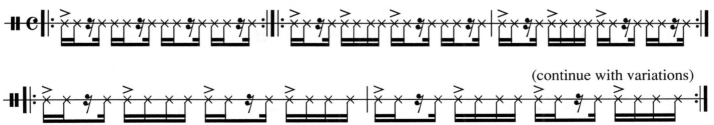

(continue with variations)

Then - Vietnam

Then are a set of four small china teacups played as a percussive instrument originally used as part of a traditional dance in the ancient Vietnamese Hue court. Then
have since found their way into many forms of Vietnamese music, due to their
delightful sound and ease of playing. Any small Chinese teacups without handles
can be used and these are readily available at import stores.

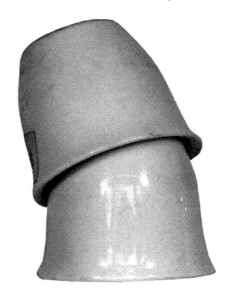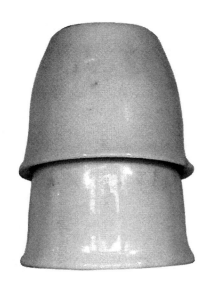

Playing the Then

Then are usually played with a pair of cups in each hand. The middle finger is placed inside
a teacup and the sides of the first and third fingers grip the sides of the same teacup just
below the rim. This teacup is inserted inside a second cup, which is being balanced on the
upturned thumb. The top teacup is lifted slightly and snapped back down percussively by
either raising the fingers as a group or by slightly dropping the thumb. This is alternated
between each hand to create the desired rhythms. To create a roll, slightly raise the top
teacup and shake the hand laterally so that the bottom teacup rattles against the top one.
Be very cautious not to raise the top teacup too much, or the bottom teacup will fall, as it is
only being held in place by the top one.

Bi Mua

(continue with variations)

100

Udu - Nigeria

The udu is a percussion pot from the Igbo people of southern Nigeria. Traditionally a woman's instrument, the udu traveled first to neighbouring tribes and then around the world to become a favourite instrument in any hand drummer's arsenal. Traditionally, udu were simple water jugs with a second hole, but now they come in a wide variety of shapes and sizes and have led to many new innovations. Usually udu are made from a light porous clay with iron or other metal mixed in to provide a better ring when hit.

Playing the Udu

Udu are held on the lap so that the top hole can be played by the left hand and the side hole by the right. The holes are struck with the palms of the hands so that a deep resonant tone is produced, and the top hole can be partially covered while the side hole is struck to change the pitch. Udu are also struck directly on the surface of the pot usually close to the side hole to create a high short tone, but advanced players find tones everywhere on the instrument. A variety of tones can be found by varying the amount the holes are closed while playing. A fun trick is to amplify the udu so that the lowest tone slowly starts to feedback, providing a long sustain.

Kaduna

101

Genggong - Bali

The genggong is the Balinese tension jaw harp made from the stem of a palm leaf. Genggong usually come in pairs with one having a slightly higher pitch, and are most often played together with the interlocking rhythms common to Balinese music, but also sometimes in a larger ensemble with suling and other gamelan instruments.

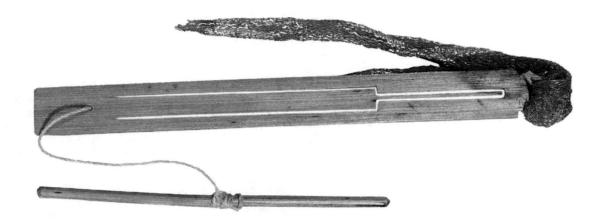

Playing the Genggong

To hold the genggong, grip the end with the cloth between the left thumb and middle joint of the index finger, and hold it directly in front of the open mouth. If there is no small bar, the string is wrapped around the index finger of the right hand, and holding the finger or bar straight, tension is placed on the string until it is taught. Quickly make a flicking motion away from the body and slightly forward, to sound the genggong. This technique usually takes quite a bit of practice to make it constant and clear. The lips and tongue change shape and position to create different tones.

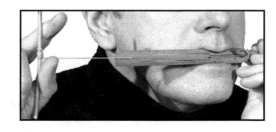

Jalan Jalan 🔘 TRACK 93

(repeat with variations)

Kouqin, Koqin, or Kouxuan - China

Koqin is the popular term for jaw harps in China, more correctly called kouqin or kouxuan, literally translating to "mouth instrument or mouth string" respectively. Most kouqin are found in the southwest part of the country played by minority peoples, the most interesting of which are the multiple jaw harps. The Naxi people have a set of four bamboo kouqin played together, comprised of three plucked and one tension instrument. Recently sets of three or four brass kouqin have come on the international market as well. Traditionally, kouqin were used for personal entertainment, in some regions played by only one person, while in other regions they were used by couples as a coded language that was part of the wooing process.

Playing the Kouqin
Playing the multiple brass kouqin takes a bit of practice. First spread the set of kouqin into a fan shape so that the lamella or tongue of each instrument is free to move. The sets are often not arranged in an ascending or descending pitch order and must be taken apart and rearranged if desired. Each instrument is plucked by a separate finger, while the set of kouqin are held in front of the mouth opened very wide, and moved up or down to center each instrument in front of the mouth as it is played. The performer's tongue and shape of the palette are changed to alter the sound of the kouqin especially to make it more vocal.

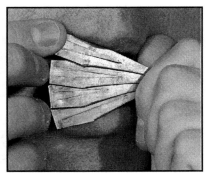

Meili CD TRACK 94

Kubing and Giwong - Philippines

The giwong is a bamboo, plucked jaw harp from Luzon, the main north island of the Philippines, and the kubing is a bamboo plucked jaw harp from Mindanao, the main southern island. Both are used to converse between young lovers, as well as for personal enjoyment. The giwong is rectangular often with small designs inscribed into the top, while the kubing has more of a handle, which is often adorned with paint or even metal.

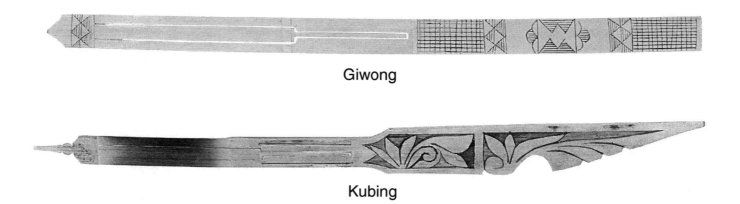

Giwong

Kubing

Playing the Giwong and Kubing
Both the giwong and kubing can be plucked either outward or inward, and the giwong can be plucked in both directions. Some performers use the tip of the index finger to pluck while others use the pad of the finger while the finger is held at right angles to the instrument. The giwong and kubing are not held between the lips, but rather are held against the lips, with the lips are pulled tight over the teeth, leaving enough room for the lamellae to pass between the lips. The tongue and palate are moved to create a wealth of tones. Both of these instruments also use a sharp intake or exhale of breath as a percussive element.

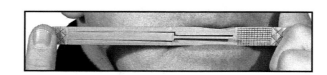

Maquinit

(continue with variations)

Berimbau - Brazil

The berimbau is a musical bow used to accompany *Capoeira*, the Brazilian martial art. Resembling its African ancestors, the berimbau is made from a long wooden branch with a metal string tied to both ends and pulled taut to create a bow. A gourd is tied close to the end on one side of the branch with the chord wrapped around the metal string and pulled tight, so that the metal string sounds two different notes when struck on either side of the chord. Berimbau have become quite popular and are found in many forms of percussive music.

Playing the Berimbau
The berimbau is held in two ways, depending where the gourd is placed on the string. If the gourd is placed about a third the way along the string, then it is held with the left hand with the last three fingers gripping the stick under the cord tying the gourd on, so that the gourd is held against the stomach. If the

gourd is placed low on the string, which is typical in the traditional Brazilian method, then the left hand holds the berimbau above the gourd while making sure the string can be reached with a finger. A coin, stone or seashell is held between the left thumb and index finger, so that it can touch the string to raise the pitch. The right hand holds a small thin stick to hit the string with, as well as a small basket rattle called *caxixi*. With the right hand, the player strikes the string with the stick and at the same time shakes the caxixi. The left hand alternately leaves the string open, touches the string lightly with the coin to make a rattling sound, or closes the string with the coin to obtain a slightly higher pitch. There are wealth of traditional rhythms, some of which can be heard on the web.

Capoeira Angola   TRACK 96   Traditional

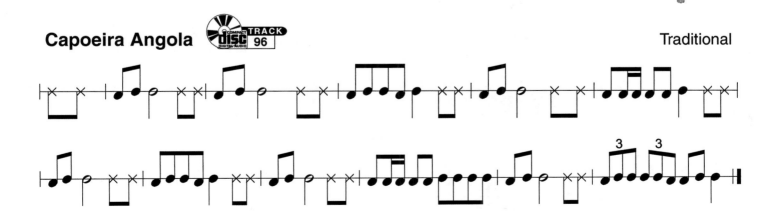

Chipendani - South Africa

The chipendani is a single string mouth bow from South Africa. It has a small thread a third the distance along the string that surrounds both the string and bow, dividing the string into two pitches, often tuned a fifth, fourth or octave apart. The chipendani has an extremely quiet sound, and is commonly used for personal entertainment. Often players will sing and play the chipendani at the same time.

Playing the Chipendani
The left hand holds the centre of the bow, so that the index finger can stop the bowstring when extended. The top of the bow is rested against the right cheek beside the mouth. The right hand alternately plucks both sides of the bowstring with a unique technique. The tips of the index finger and thumb touch to make a circle, with the bowstring inside the circle. The hand is then gently pulled away from the bow so the string slips between the thumb and finger tips effectively plucking the string. The two sides of the divided string will sound different pitches, and stopping the string with the extended left index finger can produce a third pitch.

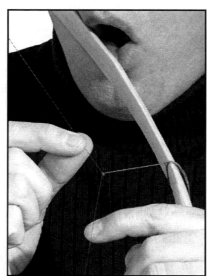

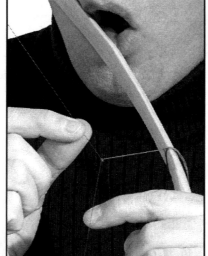

Karoo DISC TRACK 97

(continue with variations)

Kalimba - Africa

The kalimba is a *lamellaphone* made from a box resonator, on which are attached a number of metal or occasionally wooden tongues that are plucked with the thumbs. They are found in many regions of Africa in a variety of shapes, sizes and names, including *sanza* and *likembe*. In most regions, kalimba are used for personal enjoyment, played when sitting or walking. They can also be used to accompany singing. Often, there are small rattles or buzzers attached to the sides or the tongues to produce an additional rattling sound. In the West, kalimba are often referred to as thumb pianos.

Playing the Kalimba

The kalimba is held between the two hands so the thumbs are free to pluck the tongues. Often two adjacent tongues are plucked at the same time with a single thumb stroke. Some performers also use their first fingers as well. A variation is to place the kalimba on the lap and pluck with a number of fingers to obtain more chords. Usually the notes are arranged so that a scale alternates between the two hands.

Tuning the Kalimba

Kalimba are tuned by lengthening or shortening the tongues. The most common way is to tap the ends lightly and repeatedly with a small hammer or rock to the desired pitch. Caution is required not to bend the tongues, which will damage them. Most kalimba are tuned to diatonic scales but some are made to be tuned to pentatonic scales.

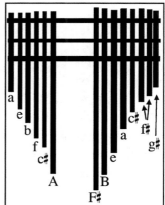

Lobeke

Mbira - Zimbabwe, South Africa

Mbira is a general name for the lamellaphones of southern Africa. They differ from those of the north in that they usually are comprised of at least three rows of tongues mounted on a small board that is then held inside a large gourd resonator. There are a number of different styles that differ in the number of tongues, the placement of the tongues and the methods of playing. Mbira are most often a solo instrument, but two or more mbira playing together are not unheard of. These are instruments of great virtuosity and are not easy to master, but they have attracted a worldwide audience, and teachers can be found in many areas in the West.

Tuning the Mbira

There are a variety of tunings for the mbira, which are determined by the instrument and the region the music comes from. The most common tuning is shown here. To adjust the tuning, slightly tap on the ends of the tongues with a small hammer or rock to raise or lower the pitch, be careful, not to bend the tongue or it will cease to sound.

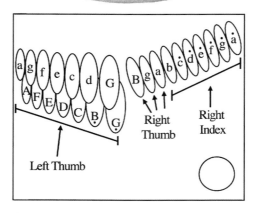

Playing the Mbira

Playing the mbira takes some practice. Usually the left two rows are always played with the left thumb. The right row is played with the right index finger except for the last three tongues on the left, which are played by the right thumb. The thumbs press down on the tongues while the finger plucks upwards. With practice this becomes quite natural. Some players insert their right little finger into the hole on the mbira to stabilize the instrument. First a student learns the basic rhythm and pattern of a piece and then learns to interpret freely.

Nhemamusasa
TRACK 98b

Traditional

Musical Glasses, Glass Harmonica - Europe

The glass harmonica is a set of wine glasses made to pitch that are stroked to produce sound. The instrument has possible roots in Persia, and a version can be seen in a woodcutting from fifteenth century Europe, but the glass harmonica did not become popular in Europe till the eighteenth century. Finer glass harmonica are made from crystal and are either chosen or made to pitch so that water does not need to be added to tune them. Ben Franklin made a modern version with glass bowls on a rotating spindle, but these instruments have a much different sound.

Playing the Musical Glasses
The glasses must be fixed to a board yet free enough to vibrate slightly. The rims of the glasses and the performer's hands must be washed and thoroughly rinsed clean with a strong detergent to remove all oils. Then they are quickly rinsed in pure vinegar to remove any further residue. Fingers moistened with water are then rubbed around the top rims of the glass to create sound. High quality glasses will instantly respond and can be played very quickly. There are many ways to arrange the glasses. Some arrangements allow up to three glasses to be played with each hand at the same time. Sometimes the rims of the glasses may need to be polished with emery cloth to obtain a better sound.

Clear Water Moon

Musical Saw - United States, Sweden

The musical saw is a thin bladed carpenter's saw that is bowed. The saw was a popular Vaudeville instrument and may have originated there and spread throughout the Americas and Europe with traveling performers. There are numerous musical saw manufactures to be found in the US and Europe, but many players still prefer to buy a very inexpensive saw from a hardware store, looking for a saw with both a good voice and good flexibility. There are a number of professional sawyers that perform a wide repertoire, ranging from popular tunes of the 1920s, to saw concerti with orchestras.

Playing the Saw
The saw handle is firmly placed between the knees while seated so that the teeth face the body and the blade is vertical. The tip of the blade is then grasped between the left thumb and fingers and bent towards the floor on the left to form a large arc (some sawyers will cut a groove close to the end of a short stick or piece of horn to create a small handle to use on the tip of the saw instead of the left thumb and fingers). Maintaining this arc, the tip is then bent towards the ceiling so that a second arch is formed and the blade is curved like the letter "s". A violin bow is held in the right hand and the saw is bowed at the top of the first arc. As the left hand increases and decreases the depth of the first arc, the top of the arc changes position and the bow must follow this to sound the changing pitches. As the left hand pushes down, the arc moves closer to the tip, and as the left hand rises, the arc moves closer to the handle, as does the bowing position. Vibrato can be achieved by shaking the right leg.

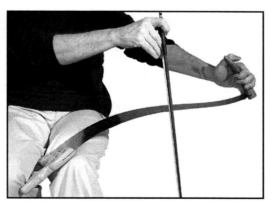

Old Bessie 🔊 TRACK 99b

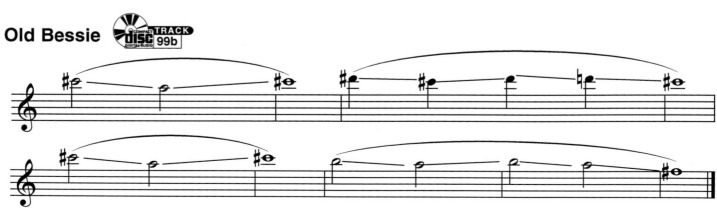

Glossary

Alapini vina - a seventh century Indian stick zither that is the forerunner of the Thai pin pia.

Anhemitonic - a scale without semitones.

Chromatic - twelve-tone scale, all the pitches possible in the western scale.

Counterpoint - two or more separate lines of music that sound together and may or may not directly relate to each other.

Diatonic - seven tone scale, consisting of five whole tones and two semitones without accidentals, e.g. in C major scale using only the white keys of the piano.

Double courses - doubled strings that are played as one string, usually tuned to the same pitch or an octave apart.

Embouchure - the position of the lips and mouth for playing wind instruments, adjusted by tightening the corners of the mouth and tensing parts of the lips.

Fifth - an interval consisting of seven semitones, often referring to the fifth tone above the tonic in a diatonic scale.

Fipple - the mouthpiece of a flute like a recorder or a tin whislte.

Fourth - an interval consisting of five semitones, often referring to the fourth tone above the tonic in a diatonic scale.

Glissandi - a large gesture moving through a series of consecutive notes like running a hand along the keys of the piano.

Harmonic - an overtone of a fundamental frequency. On a string instrument it is a high tone produced by touching a string lightly at one of its nodal points.

Hemitonic - scale with semitones.

Hocketing – a musical technique where each note of the melody is alternated between the performers.

Hua - literally "a flower", the term for a large glissando on the Chinese zheng.

Kharak - a row of bridges on the Persian santur.

Kse diev - a one string Cambodian stick zither that is related to the Thai pin pia.

Modes - in western music, a mode is one of seven arrangements of the intervals in a diatonic scale in a fixed key, e.g. Ionian (major scale), Aeolian (natural minor scale). In non-western music a mode is an arrangement of intervals available in a fixed key.

Octave - the same pitch but 8 notes higher or lower, i.e. C to c.

Ostinato - a clearly defined musical phrase that is repeated successively and persistently throughout part or all of a piece.

Overblowing - a method of blowing harder on a wind instrument to produce overtones and sounds other than the fundamental pitch. In some instruments, only these overtones are produced as the fundamental pitch cannot sound, e.g. fujara.

Pentatonic - scale with only five notes.

Portamento - a smooth sliding between pitches without distinguishing the intervening tones.

Quarter tone - one half of a semitone, common in Arabic and other non-western music.

Rokan - a tubular pick and slide made from bamboo, ivory or bone, used to play the Japanese ichigenkin or nigenkin.

Sanjo - a Korean form of solo virtuosic instrumental music.

Scale - a fixed arrangement of intervals that can be performed in any key. The interval arrangement of a major scale is tone, tone, semitone, tone, tone, tone, semitone.

Shawm - a conical double reed from the Middle East and the ancestor to the conical double reed family.

Staccato - a note played in a short, clipped manner with a rapid articulation and no sustain.

Tonic - the first note of a scale, or main note of a key.

Tremolo - a rapid repetition of a tone, or rapidly alternating between two tones.

Tsume - ivory or plastic picks used to play the Japanese koto.

Unison - "together", here referring to two strings tuned to the same pitch.

Vòi dàn - a stick made from buffalo horn found on one end of the Vietnamese dan bau. When pulled or pushed it changes the pitch of the single string attached to it.

Wah - a slang musical term, meaning to change the tonal envelope of a sound to create a vocal "wah" effect.

Yao - a tremolo played on the Chinese zheng.

Bibliography

Chinese Music Dictionary, Chinese Music Research Institute, People's Music Publishing Company, Beijing, 1985

Harvard Dictionary of Music, The Belknap Press of Harvard University Press, Cambridge MA, 1969

Korean Music, Faber Music Ltd., London, 1987

The New Grove Dictionary of Musical Instruments, Macmillan Press Limited, London, 1984

The Adungu (Arched Harp): Its Beginnings and Development Among the Alur, James K. Makubuya, MIT Music & Theater Arts, 14N-221b

www.kashaka.com

The Recordings

All pieces performed by Randy Raine-Reusch (www.asza.com) except for the following:

Balafon performed by **Fana Soro** (www.masabo.com) - Bakari, traditional.
Berimbau performed by **Eclilson de Jesus** (www.achebrasil.com) - Capoeira Angola, traditional
Biwa performed by **Wei Wang** - Introduction to Shizuka Gozen, traditional
Cajon performed by **Emad Armoush** - Flamenco Tango, traditional
Charango performed by **Rene Hugo Sanchez** (aire@flamenco.ca) - Carnaval de Tinta, traditional
Dan Bau performed by **Bich Ngoc Ho** (www.khacchi.com) - Vong Co, traditional
Dan tranh performed by **Mei Han** (www.asza.com) - Halong, R. Raine-Reusch
Djembe performed by **Fana Soro** (www.masabo.com) - Bpene, traditonal
Duduk performed by **Victor Chorobik** (www.chorobik.com) - Lament, traditional
Dumbek performed by **Emad Armoush** (aire@flamenco.ca) - Baladi, traditonal
Erhu performed by **Jun Rong** - Jasmine Flower, traditional
Fujara performed by **Victor Chorobik** (www.chorobik.com) - Nizke Tatry, traditional
Kechapi performed by **Sutrisno Hartana** - Sulu, traditional
Koni performed by **Bich Ngoc Ho** (www.khacchi.com) - On the Mountain Top, traditional
Koto performed by **Mei Han** (www.asza.com) - Meiji Shoten, R. Raine-Reusch
Mbira performed by **Blessing Mubaiwa** (www.feso.com) - Nhemamusasa, traditional
Oud performed by **Gordon Grdina** (www.sanghamusic.com) - Brown-Eyed Woman, traditional
Pandeiro performed by **Eclilson de Jesus** (www.achebrasil.com) - Samba, traditional
Pipa performed by **Wei Wang** - Lao Liu Ban, traditional
Quena performed by **Edgar Muenala** (www.nativosite.com) - Inca's Cry, traditional
Rebab Indonesia performed by **Sutrisno Hartana** - Tiga, traditional
Ruan performed by **Zhi Min Yu** - Torch Festival, traditio
Shakuhachi performed by **Joseph 'Pepe' Danza** (www.
Sitar performed by **Joseph 'Pepe' Danza** (www.pepe-n
Suona performed by **Zhong Xi Wu** - Zheng Yue Li Lai,
Tar performed by **Amir Koushkani** (www.koushkani.co
Tarka performed by **Edgar Muenala** (www.nativosite.cc
Zamponia performed by **Edgar Muenala** (www.nativosi
Zheng performed by **Mei Han** (www.asza.com) - Sprinc